C000056356

AT THE WELLSPRING

Visit our web site at
WWW.ALBAHOUSE.ORG

AT THE WELLSPRING
Jesus and the Samaritan Woman

Brother John of Taizé

ALBA·HOUSE   NEW·YORK

SOCIETY OF ST. PAUL, 2187 VICTORY BLVD., STATEN ISLAND, NEW YORK 10314

ST PAULS

Originally published in French by Ateliers et Presses de Taizé,
Taizé-Communauté, France under the title
Tout près de la source: Jésus et la Samaritaine.

Library of Congress Cataloging-in-Publication Data

John de Taizé, frère.
   [Tout près de la source. English]
   At the wellspring : Jesus and the Samaritan woman / Brother John of Taizé.
     p. cm.
   ISBN 0-8189-0892-0 (alk. paper)
   1. Bible. N.T. John IV, 1-42—Criticism, interpretation, etc. I. Title.

   BS2615.2.J59313 2001
   226.5'06—dc21

                                 00-066357

Produced and designed in the United States of America by the
Fathers and Brothers of the Society of St. Paul,
2187 Victory Boulevard, Staten Island, New York 10314-6603,
as part of their communications apostolate.

ISBN: 0-8189-0892-0

© *Copyright 2001 by the Society of St. Paul*

Printing Information:

Current Printing - first digit   1   2   3   4   5   6   7   8   9   10

Year of Current Printing - first year shown

2001   2002   2003   2004   2005   2006   2007   2008   2009   2010

BY THE SAME AUTHOR:

The Pilgrim God: A Biblical Journey
(Washington: The Pastoral Press, 1985 / Dublin: Veritas, 1990)

The Way of the Lord: A New Testament Pilgrimage
(The Pastoral Press / Veritas, 1990)

Praying the Our Father Today
(The Pastoral Press, 1992)

God of the Unexpected
(London: Geoffrey Chapman / Mowbray, 1995)

The Adventure of Holiness:
Biblical Foundations and Present-Day Perspectives
(New York: ST PAULS / Alba House, 1999)

This book is based on a series of reflections on the fourth chapter of the Gospel according to Saint John, the story of Jesus and the woman at the well. They were given as Bible introductions during the international meetings which bring tens of thousands of young adults to the French village of Taizé each year to share the life and worship of the ecumenical monastic community located there.

After a preliminary section which situates the theme of wells and water in the global context of the Hebrew Scriptures, the book follows Saint John's narrative step by step. Verses from the New Testament story are given in large print and followed by a commentary. When other Bible texts are quoted in the course of the commentary itself, they are always printed *in italics*.

In addition, **three signs** are employed to help make the layout more understandable. They indicate optional elements which periodically interrupt the main text:

▶ *placed to the left of the commentary, indicates Bible texts or references which are not part of the main argument but which complete or illustrate what was said.*

      ✔ indented on the right, refers to an explanatory note.

      ❓ likewise indented on the right, refers to questions that help make the bible story relevant today. They can be used for personal reflection or as a starting-point for a small-group discussion.

AT THE WELLSPRING

Background

The Well in the Bible

At the heart of the Christian faith

there is neither a philosophy of life nor a system of morality but a person, the man called Jesus of Nazareth. The world has always been fascinated by this figure; countless books have been written to try and analyze the secret of his appeal. On the basis of his human characteristics he could be described in many different ways—as a teacher of wisdom, for instance, or a prophet, a charismatic leader, a revolutionary, a good man. Although all of these approaches undoubtedly contain part of the truth, for believers, when all is said and done, they remain insufficient. Starting from a completely different vantage point, a key phrase at the beginning of Saint John's Gospel states the importance of Jesus for the eyes of faith:

No one has ever seen God;
the only Son,
pressed against the Father's bosom,
has made him known.
(John 1:18)

From the perspective of faith, the key to understanding Jesus is not found solely on the level of his humanity. He is the *only Son,* the one who has a unique relationship with that Mystery at the heart of existence that we call God. As a consequence, his human life reveals fully the identity of this God. That is why Saint John can refer to Jesus as the *Logos,* the Word of God who comes into the world. He is, at the heart of human history, the tangible expression and communication of the unseen God.

▶ *Read John 1:1-18*

? Who is Jesus of Nazareth for me? What Gospel texts
are most helpful for me to discover his identity?

But the expression "the Word of God" is also applied to that collection of books we call the Bible. And
we know that our Christian Bible is divided into two
parts: the Old Testament, which tells the story of the
people of Israel before the birth of Jesus of Nazareth,
and the New Testament, which recounts the life and
message of this Jesus. So the question naturally arises:
what do we need the Old Testament for? If everything
is given in Jesus Christ, cannot we simply discard the
rest? This question is not a new one; it has been asked,
often insistently, since the earliest days of the Christian
faith. What makes it even more important is the fact
that, in the eyes of many, the difference between the
two Testaments appears striking. They readily oppose
the God of the Old Testament, a fierce and bloody
warrior-god, to the God of Jesus Christ, the so-called
"god of love." Another good reason, it would seem, to
eliminate the first half of our Bibles and focus once and
for all on the essential.

If we look closer, however, we will see that in fact
things are not so simple. Understanding the relationship between the two parts of the Bible helps us better
to grasp the way in which God enters into communication with our world. To say that, in Jesus Christ, the
divine being and will are definitively revealed does not
mean that God can **only** be known through Christ. On
the contrary, through the creation of the universe and
the history of humanity from its beginnings down to
the present day, God has never ceased to communicate
in a great diversity of ways. It is not in our power to
limit God's presence to what we have understood of
it. Being Christian does not require us to refuse the
quality of revelation to anyone or anything; it simply

means believing that Jesus Christ recapitulates all that was fragmentary in other acts of revelation, clarifying them, confirming their truth and revealing their deepest significance. His person is thus the site of a discernment or, to put it in a more biblical fashion, of a judgment (in Greek *krisis*).

▶ *After having spoken to our ancestors in the old days at many different times and in many different ways through the prophets, in these last days God has spoken to us through the Son.... (Hebrews 1:1-2)*

And among all the ways in which God communicates, a unique and in some sense emblematic role is played by the tiny nation of Israel. Emblematic, because all the twists and turns of human history, with its glories and its miseries, are found there in a nutshell. Unique, because that history takes explicit shape on the basis of a relationship with the Mystery we call God. It thus offers the framework in which God's *only Son* will be born; it provides the flesh which will be the bodily expression of the Word.

▶ *The Word became flesh and dwelt among us. (John 1:14)*

In theological terms, we say that Christ **fulfilled** the Scriptures; in other words, he is the culmination that reveals the full and authentic meaning of what went before. But the same thing can be said starting from the other side: to understand Christ's identity and message correctly, they must be situated in the context of an ongoing history that encompasses them on all sides. The two parts of the Bible, therefore, complete one another; each sheds light on the other. The more we try to understand one, the more we are led to deepen our knowledge of the other.

The text we are going to examine, from the fourth

chapter of the Gospel according to Saint John, offers a
good illustration of what has just been said. It recounts
a simple meeting between a man and a woman beside
a well in Samaria, with the symbolism of water occupying a central place. Before turning to the Gospel story
itself, then, we will find it helpful to examine the
significance of these realities in the Hebrew Scriptures.

It is easy to see that after the air we breathe, water is the most precious substance for human beings on
our planet. Without water, no life can last for a very
long time. And today, in the so-called developed coun-
tries, to get water all we need to do is turn on the tap.
Water is thus generally taken for granted, almost as
much as the air around us, and as a consequence its
symbolic significance is weakened.

But in most times and places, things are far from
being that easy. Water does not arrive automatically; it
has to be sought. If you are lucky you can find it on the
surface of the earth, in rivers, lakes or springs. But in
more arid parts of the globe, such as Palestine, where
the desert is never far away, it is not as simple as that.
People are forced to dig beneath the surface to find an
underground spring. That is what we call a well.

We should thus be able to understand why, in the
world of the Bible, especially in the earlier periods, wells
were important sites. They were literally sources of life,
focal points that made possible the existence of human
beings in society. Around these key sites, a whole network of life could spring up and develop. Wells were
thus places where people gathered and, human nature
being what it is, it was not rare that they were also
places of conflict:

*[Isaac] had so many flocks and herds and servants that
the Philistines envied him. So all the wells that his father's*

servants had dug in the time of his father Abraham, the Philistines stopped up, filling them with earth. (...) Isaac reopened the wells that had been dug in the time of his father Abraham, which the Philistines had stopped up after Abraham died and he gave them the same names his father had given them. Isaac's servants dug in the valley and discovered a well of fresh water there. But the herders of Gerar quarreled with those of Isaac and said, "The water is ours!" So he named the well Esek, because they disputed with him. Then they dug another well, but they quarreled over that one also; so he named it Sitnah. He moved on from there and dug another well, and no one quarreled over it. He named it Rehoboth, saying, "Now the Lord has given us room and we will flourish in the land." (Genesis 26:14-15,18-22)

Places of conflict and sometimes places of reconciliation, springs of water create around themselves a kind of microcosm of human society made up of individual thirsts and the need to take others into account, involving generosity and egotism.

But among all the possible encounters between people that can take place around a well, there is one that takes on particular importance in the Hebrew Bible, namely, the meeting between a man and a woman. In this respect, three texts form a mini-tradition that is very useful for understanding the Gospel story of Jesus and the Samaritan woman.

The first narrative is found in chapter 24 of the Book of Genesis. Its starting-point is Abraham's desire to find a wife for his son Isaac. To accomplish this, the patriarch sends an old and trusted servant back to the country of his birth, far from the land of Canaan where he now lives. The servant stops to rest beside a well and says this prayer:

O Lord, God of my master Abraham, give me success to-
day, and show kindness to my master Abraham. See, I
am standing beside this spring, and the daughters of the
townspeople are coming out to draw water. May it be that
when I say to a girl, "Please let down your jar that I may
have a drink," and she says, "Drink, and I'll water your
camels too"—let her be the one you have chosen for your
servant Isaac. By this I will know that you have shown
kindness to my master. (Genesis 24:12-14)

A short time later, a girl named Rebekah comes
to the well with her jar to draw water. The servant asks
for a drink and things happen just as he had described
in his prayer. The girl invites him to spend the night
with her family, and to his surprise he discovers that
they are relatives of Abraham. Following a long exchange of words, Rebekah agrees to leave with the eld-
erly man to take Isaac as her husband.

In this story, there are details that recall more
specifically chapter 4 of John's Gospel. After meeting
the man at the well, *"the girl ran and told her mother's*
household about these things" (Genesis 24:28; compare
John 4:28) saying, *"This is what the man said to me"*
(Genesis 24:30; compare John 4:29). We should not
assume that these similarities are a mere coincidence.
The Christians of the first generation were mainly Jews
who were quite familiar with the Scriptures of their
people, and so it is normal that, in telling a story, they
were influenced by traditional models. This in itself is
not an indication that they invented the story in question, but simply that its form may have been deter-
mined in part by the tradition from which it came.

The well in John 4 is called "Jacob's well," and the
second story we will look at (Genesis 29:1-14) is cen-
tered on Jacob, the son of Isaac. Traveling far from
home, he stops beside a well covered with a large stone.

Some shepherds are there, and they wait for all the flocks to arrive before they roll away the stone that covers the mouth of the well and give the sheep to drink. The reason for this is not clear from the text itself: do they wait because the stone is so heavy, or rather is the well covered because it does not give much water, and so they do not share the water until all are present in order to avoid dissension?

In any event, at that moment a girl arrives with her sheep. She is Jacob's cousin Rachel. When he sees her, Jacob rolls the stone away from the well and waters the sheep that belong to his uncle Laban. He goes home with them and ends up staying there. Wishing to marry Rachel, he must first spend fourteen years in her father's house. In the end, he remains in that land for some twenty years.

Just like his descendant Jesus, Jacob offers water to an unknown woman. The link with John's Gospel becomes clearer, however, if we do not start with the narrative as it is written down in the Bible, but rather look at the way the Jews of Jesus' time told the story in their own words. Fortunately, we have documents that provide us with these versions.

> ✔ These documents are the **Targumim,** paraphrases of the Bible in Aramaic, the language of everyday life, for those who could no longer read Biblical Hebrew, as well as the **Midrashim,** commentaries or homilies explaining the books of the Bible, often by putting together different texts and weaving a new story out of them.

According to some traditions, when Jacob rolls away the stone, the water begins to gush forth and becomes a great fountain, so that from that day on there is more than enough water for everybody. This version of the story has the advantage of offering a plausible explanation for Laban's "dishonest" behavior: he wants to keep Jacob with him as long as possible, fearing that if he leaves, the water will return to the previous level and the shepherds will have to work hard once again to water their flocks.

In the light of this version of the story, the Samaritan woman's reply when Jesus promises her living water takes on new meaning: *"Are you greater than our father Jacob...?"* (John 4:12). In other words: "Are you going to perform a miracle like he did, or perhaps even do something more impressive? Just who do you think you are?"

The third account in this tradition of encounters beside a well concerns Moses (Exodus 2:15-22). Forced to flee Egypt after his unsuccessful attempt to establish justice, he stops to rest beside a well. When a group of girls, here seven sisters, come to water their flocks, they are intimidated by some shepherds. Moses comes to their rescue and then waters their sheep. Their father invites him to stay with them, and it should not surprise us that in the end Moses marries one of the daughters.

Here too, when they told the story, Jesus' contemporaries added extra details. In one version, Moses performs a miracle like Jacob's by causing water to spring up out of the well. This proves to his future father-in-law that he is indeed a descendant of Jacob. And the Jewish historian Flavius Josephus begins his account of the story in this way:

"When he came to the city Midian (...) [Moses] sat upon a certain well, and rested himself there after his laborious journey, and the affliction he had been in. It was not far from the city, and the time of the day was noon...."

✔ *Jewish Antiquities* II, ch. 11:1, translated by William Whiston.

These are details we will meet again in Saint John's Gospel (John 4:5-6). In this way, the story of Jesus and the Samaritan woman is in clear continuity with the patriarchs and Moses. As we shall see, Jesus brings to fulfillment what they prefigure on the level of the narrative itself and its literal meaning.

In addition to these stories of meetings beside a well that lead to a marriage, the theme of water takes on great importance during the Exodus experience of God's people Israel. After the Israelites leave Egypt under the guidance of Moses, they must cross the desert before reaching the promised land. The desert is by definition the place where water is lacking, and so it is there that God can be revealed unambiguously as the Wellspring of life by miraculously giving the people to drink.

▶ *Read Exodus 17:1-7 and Numbers 20:1-11. See also Isaiah 41:18; 43:20; 48:21; Psalm 78:15-16; 105:41; 114:8.*

In this respect, an enigmatic text found in the Book of Numbers takes on great importance in the later tradition:

From there they continued on to Beer, the well where the Lord said to Moses, "Gather the people together and I will give them water." Then Israel sang this song:
"Spring up, O well!
Sing about it,
about the well that the princes dug,
that the nobles of the people sank—
the nobles with sceptres and staffs."
Then they went from the desert to Mattanah,
from Mattanah to Nahaliel, from Nahaliel to Bamoth,
and from Bamoth to the valley in Moab
where the top of Pisgah overlooks the wasteland.
(Numbers 21:16-20)

What is this text about? There is a well in the desert, a song sung to the well, and a list of places the people have to pass through on their journey. At first sight, the meaning of all this is far from obvious. And yet precisely because such a text is not immediately clear, it opens up a vast field for investigation and reflection.

> ✔ Traditional Jewish exegesis has always been fascinated by such passages. The lack of clarity, of surface rationality, is heard as a call to go deeper, to look for treasures hidden beneath the surface of the text. The early Christian theologians, in their own way, walked in the footsteps of the Jewish rabbis by distinguishing the different senses of Scripture. If to us today their interpretations sometimes seem farfetched, we should not lose sight of their basic insight, which remains valuable. They understood that the meaning of the Scriptures is not exhausted by remaining on the literal level, or simply by discovering the conscious intention of the inspired author; the Bible is a gateway to the unfathomable Mystery of God.

The rabbis explained these verses in the following way. The water given by God in the desert was in fact the gift of a **well**, a well that had been dug centuries earlier by the patriarchs (the *princes* in verse 18). It was thus the very same well as that of Abraham, Isaac and Jacob. And this miraculous well accompanied the people as they journeyed in the wilderness; that is the meaning of the itinerary in verses 18b-20. In the final analysis, then, there was only one well, a miraculous spring given by God to provide water for the nation during its pilgrimage.

Basing themselves on this interpretation, some rabbis took a step further. If this is the case, they reasoned, the passage cannot be referring to a literal well that dispenses ordinary water. So they looked for an allegorical meaning to the story. They concluded that the well was in fact the Torah, the Law or Teaching given by God to Moses on Mount Sinai, a wellspring of life that constantly accompanied the people throughout its history. By the gift of the Torah, the nation was brought into contact with God's Word, with divine Wisdom. This shows us, it should be mentioned in passing, that a "spiritual" interpretation of material realities does not arise exclusively with the Gospel of Jesus Christ; it is also found in the earlier Jewish tradition.

It is clear that Saint Paul, a Jew educated as a Pharisee, was familiar with a similar tradition. Reflecting on the situation of the Israelites in the wilderness, in order to explain to the believers of Corinth that their precursors also experienced a kind of baptism, and even a Eucharist, he writes:

You should be aware, my brothers and sisters, that our ancestors were all under the cloud and all passed through the sea, and they were all baptized into Moses in the cloud and in the sea. And they all ate the same spiritual food and drank the same spiritual drink, for they drank from a spiritual rock that accompanied them; but that rock was Christ. (1 Corinthians 10:1-4)

We can see here that Paul, while also attributing a non-material significance to the story, transformed the rabbinical interpretation. For him, the spring or rock in the desert was in fact the hidden presence of Christ, who was already among his people as the Source of their life. Saint Paul thus approaches from another angle the theme which Saint John sketches out in the fourth chapter of his Gospel and which we are going to investigate.

This rapid journey through the Hebrew Bible was an attempt to situate a Gospel story by investigating the symbols of water and of the well. Source of life; gathering-place; site of conflict and reconciliation; meeting-place, notably between a man and a woman with a view to marriage; symbol of a God who takes care of his people: the well possesses a density of meaning that makes it a privileged place for understanding the relationship between God and human beings. Jesus profits from this background to transform a simple encounter into a magnificent expression of his message. He reveals in fullness what these human and biblical symbols always wished to communicate. Let us now turn to the Gospel, in order to see how it brings up to date and completes the biblical teaching concerning the gift of water.

> **?** Read Exodus 17:1-7, the story of the water from the rock in the desert, a classical example of faith being put to the test. When confronted with such a difficulty, how do the people react? How does Moses react? In a similar situation, how did I or would I react? What is God's response? What does this response tell us about God?

Foreground

Beside a Well in Samaria

John 4:1-42

1

When Jesus found out that the Pharisees had heard that he was making more disciples and baptizing more than John—though in fact Jesus himself did not do any baptizing, but rather his disciples did—he left Judea and went back to Galilee.   (John 4:1-3)

When the story begins, Jesus is on the move. In all the Gospels, Jesus almost never stays still. He spends his time journeying along the roads of Palestine, going from place to place. If he is truly the Word of God, the being who reveals fully the identity of the One he calls Abba, then we have here a somewhat unsettling image of the deity. Human beings normally conceive of God as a being who is immobile—Someone "up there," "in here" or "out there." Jesus, however, reveals to us a pilgrim God, a God who, far from waiting passively for people to come to him, takes the initiative and goes looking for human beings to invite them to journey in his company. The God of Jesus cannot be put into a box; encountering that God causes us to break out of our outer and inner prisons. That is what the woman who meets Jesus is soon going to discover.

✔ History in the Bible begins with the account of a pilgrimage. *The Lord said to Abram, "Leave your country, your people and your father's household and go to the land I will show you"* (Genesis 12:1). But if a person sets out in this way, it is because he or she is called to walk in the company of the God who takes the first step: *I am with you and will watch over you wherever you go, and I will bring you back to this land. I will not leave you until I have done what I have promised you* (Genesis 28:15).

? What does it mean for me to walk in the footsteps of the pilgrim God? What do I have to leave behind, and what lies before me?

The text also explains why Jesus is traveling. It is because of the opposition of another group, the Pharisees, a lay movement in Judaism esteemed because of the intensity of its religious commitment. The ruling circles of Israel had already looked with suspicion upon John, the man known as "the Baptizer." Their hostility was based on religious grounds, but perhaps motivated even more by political considerations. At that time, Israel enjoyed a certain limited autonomy in the framework of the Roman Empire. Any unusual commotion among the people was a threat to that fragile equilibrium and risked eliciting a brutal response from the occupying forces.

▶ *The chief priests and the Pharisees called together a council, and they said, "What can we do? That man is accomplishing many signs. If we allow him to keep on like this, everyone will start believing in him, and the Romans will come in and take over both our Holy Place and our nation." (John 11:47-48)*

And now, Jesus is starting to attract even more followers than John. This explains the authorities' concern at the success of the movement around the itinerant preacher from Galilee, and Jesus' decision to distance himself for a time from the center of the nation.

Thus, right from the start of his narrative, Saint John calls attention to the resistance to Jesus and his message, a resistance which will keep growing until it determines the end of his mission on earth. Jesus' work does not follow the customary trajectory of human success; it will achieve its end through rejection, refusal, and even apparent failure. John shows us the shadow of the cross falling over the entire ministry of Jesus from its very beginning.

2

He had to pass through Samaria. (John 4:4)

This phrase is a good example of how, in John's Gospel, apparently simple words can conceal unsuspected depths of meaning. What does this sentence mean? At first glance, it seems to refer to a physical necessity. The hills of Samaria are situated between Judea and Galilee. To go from the south to the north of the country, Jesus seemingly had no other alternative than to cross the region in between.

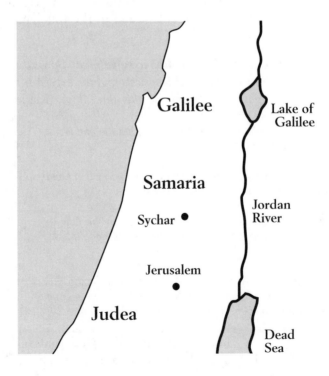

If we look more closely, however, we see that this interpretation is insufficient. For there **was**, in fact, another possibility. By going a bit further east, Jesus and his companions could have followed the Jordan valley and thus avoided the hill country. It seems that this alternative route was preferred by many of Jesus' contemporaries to keep from entering Samaritan territory. If it was not a material necessity, then, why did the Gospel-writer emphasize that Jesus **had to** pass through Samaria?

In the Gospels, the expression "to have to, must" (*deî* in Greek) can have a deeper significance. An impersonal turn of phrase used as a way to avoid pronouncing God's name, it is often used to refer to Jesus' mission in obedience to the will of God. The clearest example of this is found in the following words of Christ:

*The Son of Man **has to** suffer many things, be rejected by the elders, the chief priests and the experts in the Law, be put to death and rise after three days.* (Mark 8:31)

▶ *Jesus said, "All that **has to** happen, but the end is not yet." (Matthew 24:6)*

▶ *Jesus said to his parents, "Did you not know that I **had to** be in my Father's house?" (Luke 2:49)*

▶ *Jesus said, "Everything written of me in the Law of Moses, the Prophets and the Psalms **has to** be fulfilled." (Luke 24:44)*

▶ *Jesus said, "Just as Moses lifted up the snake in the wilderness, so the Son of Man **has to** be lifted up, so that everyone who believes in him has eternal life." (John 3:14)*

Jesus is saying here that God wants him to follow the way of the cross, not as an end in itself, of course, but in order to bring salvation to the world. Similarly, then, we can surmise that his decision to go to Samaria has a deeper significance, that it is part of the mission he has received from his Father. To evaluate this possible significance, we need to understand better who the Samaritans are and the relations they had with the Jewish people.

The Jewish people traditionally traces its origins from the twelve sons of the patriarch Jacob/Israel, the ancestors who gave their names to the twelve tribes. This view of the nation's origins is in fact a later schematization of the situation before the time of the monarchy, when Israel was a federation or association of clans unified by faith in one and the same God. Israel was a unified kingdom only for a relatively short time, during the reigns of King David and his son Solomon (1010-931 BCE). When Solomon died, two tribes alone remained faithful to the house of David and became the kingdom of the South, known as Judah. The other tribes chose their own monarchs and joined together to form the northern kingdom, called Israel, with Samaria as its capital. Two centuries later, the northern kingdom was invaded and destroyed by the Assyrians. Some of the inhabitants were deported and other populations resettled on their land.

The Samaritans are thus the descendants of the former subjects of the northern kingdom. They professed faith in the God of Israel and accepted the Books of Moses, the first five books of our Bible, but not the prophetic books written after the schism. They did not go to Jerusalem to worship, but built their own temple on Mount Garizim. The Jews, for their part, emphasized the presence of alien elements in Samaritan society. In their eyes the Samaritans were syncretists, in other words they incorporated other beliefs into their faith in the one true God.

▶ *The king of Assyria brought people from Babylon, Cuthah, Avva, Hamath and Sepharvaim and settled them in the towns of Samaria to replace the Israelites. (…) They worshiped the Lord, but they also served their own gods in accordance with the customs of the nations from which they had been brought. (…) Even while these people were worshiping the Lord, they were serving their idols. To this day their children and grandchildren continue to do as their fathers did. (2 Kings 17:24,33,41)*

At the time of Jesus, relations between Jews and Samaritans were that of feuding brothers, of which past and present history offers us so many examples. Very close in some respects, they nourished prejudices against each other and ended up mutually detesting one another.

✔ The historian Flavius Josephus (*Jewish Antiquities XX, 6,1; War of the Jews II,12,3*) mentions an altercation that took place about the year 50 between Jewish pilgrims who were going up to Jerusalem for one of the holy days and Samaritans, as a result of which one or several persons were killed. Jesus' decision to enter Samaritan territory was thus not innocuous.

It is no accident, then, that when Jesus wanted to wake up his Jewish listeners and make them think, he told a story of a man lying wounded on the roadside who is not taken care of by a Jewish priest or a Levite, but by a Samaritan who happened to be passing through.

▶ *Luke 10:29-37. Read also Luke 9:51-56 and Luke 17:11-19.*

❓ If Jesus told this parable in my situation today, who would he put in the place of the "good Samaritan" and the other characters?

At the same time, the Jewish people still felt nostalgia for their lost unity and hoped for a reunification. According to the prophets, when God would come to save the people at the end of the present age, one of the principal signs of this would be the restoration of the twelve tribes, with the north (Israel, Ephraim, Joseph) and the south (Judah) reunited under a single ruler:

The people of Judah and the people of Israel will be reunited, and they will appoint one leader and will come up out of the land, for great will be the day of Jezreel. (Hosea 1:11)

▶ *Ephraim's jealousy will vanish,*
and Judah's enemies will be cut off;
Ephraim will not be jealous of Judah
nor Judah hostile towards Ephraim.
(Isaiah 11:13)

▶ *In those days the house of Judah will join the house of*
Israel, and together they will come from a northern land
to the land I gave your ancestors as an inheritance.
(Jeremiah 3:18)

▶ *This is what the Sovereign Lord says: I am going to take*
the stick of Joseph—which is in Ephraim's hand—and of
the Israelite tribes associated with him, and join it to
Judah's stick, making them a single stick of wood, and
they will become one in my hand. (Ezekiel 37:19)

With this as a background, we can better understand how the Gospel-writer could see Jesus' coming to Samaria as a fulfillment of God's designs. For John, following in this the prophets of old, if Jesus is in fact the one sent by God into the world to save his people, that necessarily implies a gathering together and a reconciliation of all the scattered children of God.

> ▶ *[The high priest] prophesied that Jesus was going to die for the nation—and not only for the nation, but also to gather together into unity all the scattered children of God. (John 11:51-52)*

Jesus' presence in Samaria and his meeting with the Samaritans thus becomes a sign that God is gathering together his people by doing away with the centuries-old separation between North and South.

✔ Another Gospel sign that points in the same direction is Jesus' choice of twelve men *"to be with him and to be sent out"* (Mark 3:14) to proclaim the Good News *"to the lost sheep of the house of Israel"* (Matthew 10:6). By taking this step Jesus signifies that he has come to bring the Chosen People back into harmony with what it always should have been in God's eyes. His mission is to wipe out the corrosive effects of sin, which are manifested above all in division and dispersion. The nation, restored and reunited around the Twelve, will then truly be the family of God.

3

So he came to a town of Samaria called Sychar, near the plot of ground which Jacob gave to his son Joseph; Jacob's well was there. So Jesus, tired from the journey, sat down right beside the well. It was about the sixth hour.

(John 4:5-6)

Here we are in a very biblical atmosphere. Sitting beside a well, Jesus is implicitly described by John in a way which shows him to be a direct descendant of the patriarchs and Moses (see pp. 7-11). Moreover, Jesus is **tired**. In him, God enters fully into the human condition; the salvation he offers comes about through his solidarity with the negative aspects of our existence. And in an indirect fashion, the Gospel-writer shows just how far this solidarity goes. Towards the end of his Gospel, when the time comes for Jesus to be condemned to death, we read:

When he heard these words, Pilate led Jesus out and sat him down on the judgment-bench in the place called the Stone Pavement, in Hebrew Gabbatha. It was the Day of Preparation for Passover, at about the sixth hour. And he said to the Jews, "Here is your king." (John 19:13-14)

> ✔ The Greek text of John 19:13 is ambiguous; it could also mean that **Pilate** sat down on the judge's bench. But this reading, at first sight more logical, is ultimately less satisfying. See Ignace de la Potterie, *The Hour of Jesus: the Passion and Resurrection of Jesus According to John* (New York: Alba House, 1990, p. 83).

Jesus is sitting down; it is the sixth hour (noon). In this way, by means of a subtle allusion to the Passion narrative, Saint John links the story we are investigating to the definitive gift of himself that Jesus will eventually make by dying on the cross, an act that will recapitulate the meaning of his entire existence. This is John's way of informing us that everything Jesus is about to do will be possible solely because of this act of self-giving which knows no bounds.

> ❓ What other examples of Jesus' solidarity with our human condition do we find in the Gospels?

4

A woman of Samaria comes to draw water.
(John 4:7a)

Just as in the stories from the Hebrew Scriptures, as soon as someone stops beside a well, that person is joined by one or more others. If we compare the person who now enters into a dialogue with Jesus with the one in the previous chapter, we see how skillfully John has constructed his Gospel. In chapter three, Jesus had a conversation with a certain Nicodemus—a Jew, a man, a respected member of his people. He came at night to visit Jesus (John 3:2). Here, Jesus enters into a relationship with a Samaritan, a woman and, we have reason to believe, someone not held in very high esteem by her peers. Moreover, she comes at noon. In fact, the time of day she goes to the well is the first indication of her marginal status. In a warm country like Palestine, a task like going to fetch water would generally be performed early in the morning or at dusk, when it is cooler. By coming to the well at noon, when the sun is at its zenith, the woman is practically certain not to encounter anyone else. Although it is not emphasized in the story, we thus have some reason to believe that this woman did not enjoy a positive reputation in the society to which she belonged. It is not unlikely that she would have been characterized as a "sinner," a term that in those days had more social and less ethical significance than it does for us. It referred primarily to a person rejected or despised on account of the life he or she led, an "outsider."

Nicodemus (ch. 3)	Samaritan woman (ch. 4)
Jew	Samaritan
man	woman
prominent (has a **name**)	undistinguished (no **name**)
respected	in disrepute ("sinner")
comes at night	comes at noon

So Jesus first meets a Jew, a man, someone at the center of the life of his society, and then a Samaritan, a woman, someone at the edge of her society. By this play of opposites, the Gospel-writer tells us something important right from the outset, namely, that Jesus comes for all; nobody is excluded from the life he wishes to offer. No social category, philosophy of life or lifestyle makes someone unsuitable for a relationship with him. Each and every being whom the Father places in his path offers him a unique opportunity to fulfill his mission, as if he had come for that person alone.

5

Jesus said to her, "Give me to drink." His disciples had gone off into the town to buy provisions.

(John 4:7b-8)

The Gospel-writer notes that the disciples have already left the scene, so Jesus is alone with the woman. Here too, the theme of hunger makes its appearance for the first time; this theme, complementary to that of thirst, will be taken up again later on, in verses 31-34. We should note in passing that at this stage of the action the relationship between Jews and Samaritans is exclusively **commercial**. There is no mention of sharing or of hospitality; the disciples have to buy the food they need.

With the scene set in this way, Jesus takes the initiative by uttering a short phrase which seems of little import but is in fact full of meaning: he asks for a drink. By these three words in Greek (*dós moi peîn*), the newness of God explodes into the settled life of a small Samaritan town.

Let us first consider the meaning of these words for Jesus himself. He is thirsty. Here we receive another indication of his solidarity with the human condition and, more specifically, with God's people, who had experienced thirst in the course of their pilgrimage through the wilderness towards the promised land.

▶ *They camped at Rephidim, but there was no water for the people to drink. So they quarreled with Moses and said, "Give us water to drink." Moses replied, "Why do you quarrel with me? Why do you put the Lord to the test?" But the people were thirsty for water there, and they grumbled against Moses. They said, "Why did you bring us up out of Egypt to make us and our children and livestock die of thirst?" (Exodus 17:1-3)*

In addition, these words point ahead to the future. On the cross, just before he dies, Jesus will say, *"I am thirsty"* (John 19:28). Here we have, once again, a kind of foreshadowing of the definitive gift of his life which Jesus is going to make. And we should not forget that, in the Scriptures and in the rabbinical commentaries, water can take on a metaphorical significance. It is not surprising, therefore, that this is true as well for hunger and thirst. The following oracle from the prophet Amos is particularly clear in this regard:

The days are coming, declares the Sovereign Lord,
when I will send a famine through the land—
not a famine of food or a thirst for water,
but a famine of hearing the words of the Lord.
(Amos 8:11)

The rest of this story will show us that, by making human thirst his own, Jesus reveals all of its dimensions. He enables us to discover unsuspected depths in the desire that wells up in us.

> **?** What am I thirsting for—for myself, for others, for the Church, for the world? Is God looking for something from me? Are these longings able to be fulfilled?

Jesus' question also has an important meaning for his relationship with the other person. The woman's reply and the disciples' reaction when they return (John 4:27) clearly manifest that Jesus is doing something out of the ordinary. By addressing this unknown woman, he sets in motion a movement of reconciliation that transforms several different domains of human life.

First, **reconciliation between Jew and Samaritan**. What we have already said about the relationship between these two groups is sufficient to explain the importance of this step. In the eyes of Jesus, the hereditary enemy is simply a potential sister or brother. In him, God comes into the world to gather his people together, to restore its broken unity.

Second, **reconciliation between man and woman**. It is significant that, when the disciples return, what surprises them most is not that Jesus is talking with a Samaritan. They are even more astonished to see him conversing with a woman. In the world of the Bible just as in most human societies down to the present day, men and women do not only have different roles; the relationship is also an unequal one. More often than not, women are classed with children as second-class citizens; they do not take part fully in public life. In Israel at the time of Jesus, for example, only boys learned Hebrew so that they could read the Bible. The well-known story of Martha and Mary, the two sisters who were friends of Jesus, contains a noteworthy detail in this respect.

▶ *Read Luke 10:38-42*

We read that *Mary,… sitting at the Lord's feet, was listening to him speak.* In those days, the disciples of a rabbi generally sat on the ground at the feet of their teacher in order to receive instruction from him. Mary is thus described in the typical attitude of a disciple, something not at all common in that time and place. Here as elsewhere, Jesus shows surprising freedom in the way he behaves towards the women of his time. He is fully present to them and takes them very seriously, as we shall see in the encounter we are investigating.

At the same time, it should be mentioned that the Bible is far from being a mere witness to discrimination against women. Its pages are filled with examples of women of faith worthy of emulation. In addition, there is an aspect of the biblical mentality that makes it difficult for us to understand situations such as these correctly. The Bible does not focus on individuals but rather on beings-in-relation. What interests the inspired authors is less the woman or man taken in themselves than the place which that woman or man occupies in the network of mutual relationships that make up the life of society—the couple, the family, the clan, the nation. This way of looking at things sets the "inequality" of certain groups or classes in a different light, for their value is not primarily a function of their selves detached from others and taken in isolation, as is the case in a society that exalts the individual, but flows from the fact that they are fulfilling their social role correctly.

In fact, the couple (man-woman) is so important for the world of the Bible that it becomes one of the key images to express the relationship between the Lord and the people he made his own. The prophets of Israel generally used this image to criticize the behavior of their contemporaries. They compared the rebellious nation to a wife unfaithful to her husband

▶ *Read Hosea 2:4ff; Ezekiel 16; Jeremiah 2:20-25; 3:1-3*

or to men who neglect their own wives and run after other women.

▶ *Your children have forsaken me*
and sworn by gods that are not gods.
I supplied all their needs,
yet they committed adultery
and thronged to the houses of prostitutes.
They are well-fed, lusty stallions,
each neighing for another man's wife....
(Jeremiah 5:7-8)

But the positive face of this image is never completely absent, for example in the stories beside the well that we examined at the beginning of this book. Every marriage in Israel is a concrete reminder of the covenant between God and his people, a way of reliving the promise made to Abraham.

▶ *The word of the Lord came to Abram in a vision: "Do*
not be afraid, Abram. I am your shield, your very great
reward." But Abram said, "O Sovereign Lord, what can
you give me since I remain childless...?" And Abraham
said, "You have given me no children; so a servant in my

*household will be my heir." Then the word of the Lord
came to him: "This man will not be your heir, but a son
coming from your own body will be your heir." He took
him outside and said, "Look up at the heavens and count
the stars—if indeed you can count them." Then he said
to him, "So shall your offspring be." Abram believed the
Lord, and he credited it to him as righteousness. (Genesis 15:1-6)*

Seen in this context, Jesus' request of the woman
is the anticipation of a new world where men and
women live together in harmony and reciprocity, a kind
of return to Eden.

▶ *Read Genesis 2:18-25*

But it is even more: a sign of God's coming in order to
reconcile wayward humanity to himself. Seen against
the background of the biblical image of the couple, the
scene beside a well in Samaria evokes this reconciliation, which has as its ineluctable consequence reconciliation among human beings.

And this leads us to a third dimension of the reconciliation accomplished by Jesus. It involves a coming together between someone who comes in the name
of the Lord and someone who is apparently far from
God, **between the Holy One and sinners**. We have
noted that this woman is discreetly presented as a "sinner": although this aspect is not emphasized too strongly
here, it is fully in harmony with the Gospel message in
its entirety and the stupefying image of God which Jesus
reveals. Like a physician, Jesus does not come for those
who are well but for sick people in need of healing.

▶ *Jesus said, "Healthy people do not need a doctor; sick
ones do. I have not come to call the upright, but sinners."
(Mark 2:17)*

It is not people convinced of their integrity who have special access to him, but rather those who are aware of their shortcomings and their need for help.

▶ *Read Luke 18:9-14, the parable of the Pharisee and the tax-collector.*

In a word, the God of Jesus is a God of **forgiveness**, the shepherd who goes looking for the lost sheep, the one concerned above all with restoring a broken relationship.

▶ *Jesus said, "If one of you had a hundred sheep and lost one, would you not leave the ninety-nine in the wilderness and go looking for the lost one until you found it? And when you found it, you would carry it home on your back full of joy. When you got there, you would call your friends and neighbors and say to them, 'Come celebrate with me, because I have found that sheep of mine that was lost!' I tell you that there will be more joy in heaven over one sinner who changes his ways than over ninety-nine upright persons who have no need of repentance." (Luke 15:4-7)*

If we look at Jesus' dialogue with the Samaritan woman from this perspective, it is striking to see how this "forgiveness" is expressed. God's forgiveness is in fact something other than what we imagine; it goes far beyond what human beings mean when they use the word.

▶ *...Let them turn to the Lord, and he will have mercy on them, and to our God, for he will freely pardon. For my thoughts are not your thoughts, neither are my ways your ways, declares the Lord. (Isaiah 55:7-8)*

In human life, forgiveness is far from self-evident and it is not rare that, even when it is offered, it leads to a subtle humiliation of the one who is forgiven. Their

disreputable behavior is emphasized, whereas the good-
ness and magnanimity of the person who deigns to for-
give, in spite of being wronged, is brought to the fore.

God's forgiveness, though, does not work in that
way. When he enters into a relationship with the Samaritan woman, Jesus takes the lower place right from
the start. His words should not be understood as an
order or demand; they are a humble request. He comes
to the woman with empty hands, looking for something
that she alone is able to give. She has a bucket while
he has not, and so is apparently in a position of force.
Jesus therefore begins by lowering himself, and as a
consequence the woman is raised up. In other words,
Jesus reveals her human dignity: he needs her, and she
has something she can give him. In behaving this way,
Jesus also shows in what true human dignity consists.
It is not a matter of how much we own, or the power
we can exercise over others, but rather in our ability to
give, in the final analysis to give ourselves. By his request, Jesus establishes his partner right from the start
as someone truly capable of collaborating with him. It
is this collaboration which will develop and grow deeper
in the verses that follow.

> **?** What divisions do I see around me? What can I do to
> put into practice the reconciliation that Christ brings? How
> can I make sure that when I ask for or offer forgiveness, it
> does not lead to humiliating the other person but rather
> emphasizes their dignity?

6

So the Samaritan woman said to him, "How can you, a Jew, ask me, a Samaritan woman, for a drink?" (Jews do not associate with Samaritans.) (John 4:9)

Here we have the Samaritan woman's first reply. Confronted with Jesus' request, she had several different options. She could, for example, have fled in fear at encountering someone, especially a strange man. Or she could have expressed, by word or by deed, her annoyance at the request. But she did neither of these things. Instead, she showed her **astonishment**.

This is in fact a significant response. A common reaction in the Gospels is for Jesus' hearers to express their surprise at something he does or says.

▶ *The Gospels contain at least forty examples of this. For example Matthew 8:27; 9:33; Mark 10:24,26; 12:17; Luke 4:36; 5:26; John 7:15.*

If such a reaction is not in itself faith, it is nonetheless an important stage on the road to belief. Experiencing astonishment means being open to something new. When we are surprised, we implicitly realize that our ordinary way of relating to the universe is no longer completely viable. And when we are aware of the insufficiency of our current worldview and open to something else, we can welcome another Reality into our lives. In this sense, the attitude diametrically opposed to faith is not hesitation or even doubt, but rather the conviction that I already have all the answers. Lulled

to sleep by this certainty, I shut myself in and slowly
my inner life shrinks; I become impermeable to the
unsettling Newness of God.

> ✔ It is true that doubt is an obstacle to faith when it be-
> comes systematic. But upon closer investigation, we can
> see that such systematic doubt in fact conceals a preten-
> sion to certain knowledge, a secret complacency. It is as
> if we were affirming, "I am certain that trust placed in
> another person will always be disappointed."

Far from hiding behind an arrogant self-
sufficiency, then, the Samaritan woman expresses her
surprise. What is the meaning of this man's behavior,
in a world where divisions between people—reinforced
by the laws of religious purity—are the rule and not the
exception?

7

Jesus said to her in reply, "If you knew what
God gives, and who is saying to you 'Give me
to drink,' you would have been the one to ask,
and he would have given you living water."

(John 4:10)

The woman's reply enables Jesus to take a further step
forward. In this story, one of the few true dialogues we
find in John's Gospel, it is striking to note to what extent Jesus profits from the smallest opening his partner
gives him to help her to go further along the road to
Life. As a starting-point, he invites her to a radical

change in her way of thinking. The Greek term often used in the New Testament for this reversal is the word *metanoia* (literally: change of mind), usually translated by "repentance" or "conversion" but indicating more exactly in this context the radical reorientation of priorities which accompanies an encounter with the living God. Although the word itself is not used here, Jesus is proposing to her a veritable *metanoia*, which is characterized by the change from "giving" to "receiving." As she goes further on the road along which Jesus wishes to lead her, the woman will discover that there comes a time when it is more essential to ask and to receive than to give.

What makes this reversal possible is a new understanding of God brought about by a discovery of the true identity of the person speaking to her. "If you knew what God gives":

> ✔ The Greek term translated here by the verb "to know" is used not just for information but also for **persons**. "God's gift" is not an object, but an inner transformation that is the consequence of a relationship, a sharing of life. Everything in God is personal.

the gift points back to the giver. When she comes to know Jesus, the One sent from the Father, the Samaritan woman will know God as he really is. She will know him as Giver, as the Wellspring of life.

The notion of God as Giver may seem self-evident. If we recognize that we are creatures, does it not follow that all we have and all we are come from the Creator, that we possess nothing of ourselves? Nothing could be more obvious, and yet is it not also true that most of the time the image of God that arises spontaneously from our depths is not that of a Giver? People ordinarily assume that to be religious means doing something for God: praying, keeping the commandments, going to church.... As a consequence, God is essentially viewed as someone who asks for something, and religion is a duty, one more effort required of us.

The message of Jesus is "good news" (*euangelion*) precisely because it transforms this customary image of the deity and places at the center the notion of God as Giver. This is clearly expressed in that well-known text from Saint John:

For God so loved the world
*that he **gave** his only Son,*
so that whoever believes in him would not perish
but have eternal life.
(John 3:16)

God is Love

▶ *1 John 4:8,16*

and shows this love by giving what is most precious, his only Son, in order to give us life in fullness. And Jesus' own life is characterized by self-giving,

▶ *The Son of Man did not come to be served but to serve,*
*and to **give** his life as a ransom for the many. (Mark 10:45)*

recapitulated in his consenting to an atrocious death in order to give himself to the very end. To show clearly that this death was in no way an accident or a failure, but rather the perfectly adequate expression of the meaning of his life, Jesus "explained" it by a symbolic gesture during his last meal:

*And while they were eating he took bread and, when he had said the blessing, broke it and **gave** it to them, say-ing, "This is my body." And taking a cup and giving thanks, he **gave** it to them, and they all drank from it. And he* *said to them, "This is my blood of the covenant, which will be shed for the many." (Mark 14:22-24)*

The Eucharist is the translation into sacramental terms of a life that has become Gift, that reveals God as the ultimate Giver.

? What helps me to remember that God wants to fill me with gifts? Have I experienced in my life the truth that what God asks for, God gives? When and how?

And so, during a conversation beside the well of Jacob, Jesus explains to an unknown woman that by knowing him, she will know God in a new way that will turn her life upside down. She will discover that beyond anything she can do by her own efforts, she is called simply to accept the gift which God wants to give her, and to do this concretely by asking for it.

And what is this gift? Jesus gives us a preliminary definition by speaking of "living water." Here we have a typically Johannine play on words, for the most straightforward meaning of this expression is what we call in English "running water." In the first place, then, living water is simply the opposite of stagnant water in a cistern; it is a river or a spring. The woman obviously assumes that Jesus is talking about that kind of water, but the reader who remembers the importance of the term "life" in the Johannine writings may already suspect that he is referring to something much deeper. Living water is in fact "the water of life," water that gives true Life, the ultimate goal of God's designs for creation.

▶ *Jesus said, "I have come that they may have life, and have it to the full." (John 10:10)*

8

She said to him, "Sir, you have no bucket and
the well is deep. Where then do you have this
living water from? You are not greater than
our father Jacob, are you? He gave us this well,
and drank from it himself, together with his
sons and his flocks."   (John 4:11-12)

> ✔ The Greek word *kyrios* can be translated either by "sir"
> or "lord." Here it is undoubtedly another small example
> of "Johannine irony." The woman unwittingly confesses
> Jesus as the risen Lord. Moreover, in the Greek transla-
> tion of the Hebrew Scriptures, the title *Kyrios* is used es-
> pecially for God, to translate the Hebrew *YHWH* or
> *Adonai.*

Now it is the woman's turn to speak up. Her astonishment turns into **curiosity**. It is clear that she has char-
acter. She does not acquiesce passively, but wants to
know exactly how Jesus is going to come up with this
remarkable water in spite of the apparent impediments.

> ✔ In Luke 1:34, Jesus' mother shows a similar inner free-
> dom and mettle at the angel Gabriel's announcement. We
> would do well not to mistake a trusting openness for pas-
> sivity.

It is not easy to judge the tone of her questions. Is she
skeptical, or simply still unable to see what Jesus is driv-
ing at? In any case, the important thing is that she continues the dialogue; her attitude shows that she is ready
and willing to head out toward deeper waters.

The Samaritan woman puts her finger right away on the **poverty** of Jesus. Apparently destitute, he has no visible means to draw water. Here we are brought face to face with one of the major themes of the Gospel: when God enters the world to give Life to human beings, he does not generally do so by spectacular gestures, using resources that are out of the ordinary, inaccessible to most of us. On the contrary, the Son of God comes as a humble servant;

▶ *Jesus said to his disciples, "I am in your midst as one who serves" (Luke 22:27). See also Matthew 12:15-21 and John 13:4-5.*

his strength is expressed in human weakness.

▶ *Read 1 Corinthians 1:17-31*

In order to save humankind, he chooses the road of an ignominious death, abandoned by all. And since he takes the lowest place, from now on nobody is too low to encounter God. So it is fitting that here Jesus will give the living water to the woman starting from his human limits and indigence. In him, what seems impossible becomes possible.

? Have I personally had experiences of God's power expressed in human weakness or in apparent impossibilities?

Next, the woman wants to know where the water Jesus promises her will come from. Here too, Saint John reveals unsuspected depths in an apparently commonplace expression. *Where do you have it from...?* In this Gospel, the term "where from" is used to express the identity of Jesus by means of a question concerning his origins, the source of his life. After hearing his teaching, the inhabitants of Jerusalem express their disbelief:

Could it really be that the authorities have recognized that he is the Messiah? But we know where this fellow is from, whereas when the Messiah comes, no one will know where he is from. (John 7:26b-27)

▶ We know that God spoke to Moses, but we do not know where this fellow is from. (John 9:29; see also 6:42)

But Jesus replies:

So you know me and you know where I am from, do you? Yet I have not come on my own, but the one who sent me is true, and you do not know him. (...) Even though I give testimony about myself, my testimony is true, because I know where I have come from and where I am going, whereas you do not know where I come from and where I am going. (John 7:28; 8:14)

The people think they know Jesus because they are familiar with his human origins. For them he comes from Nazareth, from Mary and Joseph, and so on. But for the Gospel-writer, these facts do not reveal his true identity, for in fact Jesus comes from God, in other words from "heaven," or from "the One who sent him."

▶ God: John 3:2; 8:42; 13:3; 16:27,30; 17:8; cf. 7:29
Heaven: John 3:13,31; 6:38,41,51,58
The One who sent me: John 6:38; 7:28-29; 8:42; 17:8

Thus John uses the expression "where from" to pose the question of Jesus' identity and to indicate that it cannot be comprehended from a strictly human point of view. In the fourth Gospel this theme leads to a tragic conclusion, culminating as it does in the question of Pontius Pilate when he interrogates Jesus, "Where are you from?" (John 19:9), and the silence of Jesus in reply. Since the Roman governor is not open to the truth, words no longer have any power to communicate.

By using the expression "where from," then, Saint John implies that behind the practical question "how?" lies hidden a much more essential question, that of the **identity** of the one who offers living water. And the Samaritan woman replies indirectly to that second question with another question which expresses her disbelief while leaving the door open to further developments. Basically she says, "Who do you think you are? You don't mean to say that you are going to perform a more impressive miracle than our ancestor, the great patriarch Jacob, who caused fountains of water to gush forth from this well centuries ago!" (see p. 10). Here we encounter in fact the second implicit reply given by the woman to the question "Who is this man?" First of all, *you are a Jew* (v. 9) and now *you are not greater than our father Jacob, are you?* This theme will continue to undergo an important progression in the course of the narrative.

9

Jesus replied to her, "Anyone who drinks this water will be thirsty again. But whoever drinks the water I will give will never be thirsty again." (John 4:13-14a)

Jesus profits from the curiosity of his partner, a sign of her openness and her desire to understand more, to provide her with more information about the "living water" he can give. Already by now it should be clear to the reader, if not to the woman, that Jesus is not speaking about normal, material water. This water has the amazing property of quenching one's thirst definitively, of giving all that is necessary for life. We still need to understand, however, in what way all who drink this water will never be thirsty again—there is a nuance in the text that has to be made explicit.

There are two different ways in which a person's thirst can be taken away once and for all. In the first place, this could mean that someone will never again experience thirst, that they will undergo a change in their makeup so that they will no longer need to drink. Spontaneously, that is probably how most people would understand the meaning of Jesus' words. But these words can have yet another meaning. They can express the fact that, although still experiencing the desire to drink, human beings will always have at their disposition the means of quenching their thirst, so that their desire will never be frustrated. Upon reflection, we can see that it must be this second possibility that Jesus is referring to, for he goes on to explain that the water he gives will become a spring within the person, a source of water permanently available and thus able to quench thirst at every moment. This nuance is not without importance, for it means that God's gift does not extinguish the innate longing of human beings, their deepest desire, but rather liberates it. Jesus thus implicitly states that human longing is not illusory but points to a deeper dimension of reality; it is **revelatory**. By placing deep within them the yearning for greater being and life, God is not playing games with his creatures. God can respond to this thirst, wants to do so, will do so. And so the words of Jesus are not at all in contradiction with another passage, found in the Book of Sirach where, in portraying Wisdom by means of the image of food and drink, it is said that

Those who eat of me will hunger for more,
and those who drink of me will thirst for more.
(Sirach 24:21)

But in our story, this thirst that can never be satisfied will grow stronger and become manifest through an encounter with the inexhaustible Wellspring.

10

"No, the water I give that person will become in them a spring of water gushing forth to eternal life." (John 4:14b)

Jesus says that this water is "gushing forth to eternal life." A translator's job is not easy: in all of the versions, some liberty is taken with this phrase so that it will sound right. But this procedure keeps us from penetrating the text in all of its depth. For the verb translated as "to gush forth" or "to well up" is in fact a term not normally applied to water. It most often refers to human beings or animals. A literal translation would be "to leap up" or "to bound."

If this is the case, we are justified in asking what Saint John has in mind by writing about water that leaps up. True, his Greek vocabulary is rather meager, so it may be that the expression is merely due to a lack of familiarity with the language. Perhaps he used a word that gave a more or less approximate rendering of the idea he wanted to communicate, without attempting to be exact. But before concluding that this is in fact the case, we should see whether we can find a positive meaning for the choice of this term.

First of all, let us recall the rabbinical interpretation of the passage in chapter 21 of the Book of Numbers dealing with the water in the desert (see pp.11-13). Since it spoke about a well that accompanied the people during their pilgrimage over hill and dale, it was in some sense a well that "bounded." So here, once again, the water which Jesus gives is in continuity with the miraculous water—material or spiritual—which God wished to give his people down through the ages. Furthermore, a prophecy from the Book of Isaiah sheds light in another way on the connection between the gift of water and the act of leaping. Speaking of the age to come when God will be fully present in the world, the prophet cries out:

Then will the lame leap like a deer,
and the mute tongue shout for joy.
Water will gush forth in the wilderness
and streams in the desert.
(Isaiah 35:6)

▶ *Why was it, O sea, that you fled, O Jordan, that you*
turned back, you mountains, that you skipped like rams,
you hills, like lambs? Tremble, O earth, at the presence
of the Lord, at the presence of the God of Jacob, who
turned the rock into a pool, the hard rock into springs of
water. (Psalm 114:5-8)

Here the prophet enumerates two main signs of God's coming: first of all miracles of healing, including *the lame leaping like a deer*, and second, the desert that is transformed into a garden by the gift of water. It is not impossible that Saint John, by using the verb "to leap" in speaking about water, wanted to combine these two signs in order to show us discreetly that, in Jesus, God visits his people to offer them the long-promised salvation.

> ✔ The same verb is found in Acts 3:8 and 14:10, where it describes the effect of the new Life on the bodies of the lame; in this way the prophecies of old are finally fulfilled.

Before going further with our commentary on this story, we should stop and offer a preliminary answer to a question that lies at its heart. To what does the symbol of the living water promised by Jesus refer? This question does not imply that here Jesus is speaking **allegorically**, in the sense that the image of water simply replaces another reality which for some reason he does not wish to name directly. Such an assumption is unnecessary, because Jesus' words possess a fullness of meaning in themselves; they spring from the One who is God's Word made flesh, the inexhaustible expression of ultimate Reality. The different "interpretations" of the living water should rather be seen as approaches that help us grasp more clearly a reality which remains incapable of being described exhaustively, in theological terms a **mystery**.

With this caveat in mind, what realities of faith can we relate to the symbol of living water? We have seen that in their commentaries on Scripture, our Old Testament, the rabbis sometimes gave a spiritual meaning to water: it could refer to God's Word, the Torah revealed to Moses on Mount Sinai as a wellspring of life for the nation. A verse from the Book of Proverbs carries this line of interpretation further:

*The teaching of the wise is a fountain of life
turning people from the snares of death.*
(Proverbs 13:14)

We should not forget that in the Bible, Wisdom comes from God and ultimately tends to be identified with the Torah:

▶ *Wisdom praises herself,
and tells of her glory in the midst of her people. (…)
"I came forth from the mouth of the Most High,
and covered the earth like a mist.
I dwelt in the highest heavens,
and my throne was in a pillar of cloud. (…)
Then the Creator of all things gave me a command,
and my Creator chose the place for my tent.
He said, 'Make your dwelling in Jacob,
and in Israel receive your inheritance.'" (…)
All this is the book of the covenant of the Most High God,
the law that Moses commanded us
as an inheritance for the congregations of Jacob.
(Sirach 24:1,3-4,8,23; see also 15:1; Baruch 3:9-4:4)*

And so, an initial interpretation of the living water offered by Jesus, following in the direct line of the Hebrew Scriptures, would see it as Jesus' teaching in word and deed, by which he communicates to human beings the identity of God and God's plans for creation. In a word, it refers to the **revelation** of the Father which comes to us through his only Son.

▶ *No one has ever seen God; the only Son, pressed against
the Father's bosom, has made him known. (John 1:18)*

John's Gospel, however, provides a second interpretation of the living water, one that is different from but complementary to the first. During the Feast of Tabernacles in Jerusalem, Jesus speaks the following words in public:

> On the last day of the feast, the great day, Jesus stood
> up and cried out: "Let whoever is thirsty come to me and
> drink, whoever believes in me. As Scripture says, from
> deep within him will flow rivers of living water."
> (John 7:37-38)

And the Gospel-writer gives this commentary:

> He was speaking about the Spirit which those who believed
> in him were going to receive, for there was not any Spirit
> yet, because Jesus had not yet been glorified. (John 7:39)

The text is referring to the definitive gift of the
Holy Spirit which results from the "glorification" of
Jesus, an expression which John uses to refer to his
death and resurrection, considered as two faces of one
and the same reality. That is why the Gospel-writer
accords so much importance to the water which flows
from Jesus' side when he dies on the cross.

▶ *...one of the soldiers pierced his side with a lance, and
immediately blood and water came out. The one who saw
it has given witness—and his witness is true, and that one
knows that he speaks the truth—so that you too might
believe. (John 19:34-35)*

In the Gospel-writer's eyes, what happens on the cross
is the sign that the promise has been fulfilled. By this
gift of his life (his "blood"), Jesus becomes a spring of
living water for the entire human family; he communicates definitively the reality of the living God by giving the Holy Spirit *without measure* (John 3:34).

11

The woman said to him, "Sir, give me that water, so I will never be thirsty and never have to come back here to draw water." (John 4:15)

In her turn, the Samaritan woman now takes a big step forward. Although she does not yet fully understand where Jesus wants to lead her, she does not give up the game but remains open and tries to advance as best she can. She moves from astonishment and simple curiosity to the discovery and the expression of her thirst. All distance is finally done away with: she no longer maintains the attitude of an observer who is still not sure whether she can dare to place her trust in the words she hears. By asking for the water, she commits herself with respect to Jesus.

Jesus had begun the conversation by speaking of his own thirst (*Give me to drink*, v. 7) and now their encounter calls forth from the woman almost the same exact words: *Give me that water....* The two are now united in the discovery of a common thirst. Is there any other way for God to make us aware of our unlimited openness to being and our aspiration to a fulfillment, than by revealing his own? In short, only love can engender love.

Without intending to, the Samaritan woman gives us an excellent definition of prayer, namely, **discovering and expressing one's deepest longing**. It is true that her prayer is only in its early stages, for she still sees everything from a self-centered perspective. She thinks primarily of her own individual comfort (*so I will never be thirsty...*, v. 15), and is far from suspecting all the dimensions of that thirst and how far it can take her. Nevertheless, by her request she has taken an important step forward. She is no longer hiding behind an attitude that purports to be objective. Aware of her thirst, she is now an active participant. And Jesus is patient. Although he knows that she still has a long road before her, he has confidence in the process that has been set in motion. It is a great help never to forget that God is always more patient with us than we are with ourselves. Overflowing with compassion, he is more aware than we are of both the resistances within us and the fundamental intention of our hearts.

? Do the longings and desires within me have a place in my dialogue with God? What Bible texts, what images of God facilitate a free and trusting prayer?

The longing of his partner having thus been brought to light, Jesus can now begin a new stage in his dialogue with her. He does so by means of some disconcerting words, which on first hearing are nearly incomprehensible.

12

He said to her, "Go call your husband and come back here." (John 4:16)

It is not so easy to understand the link between the woman's request for water and Jesus' directive to go get her husband. Does Jesus only give living water to married couples? Is an unwed woman not allowed to receive this gift?

In our examination of the Hebrew Scriptures, we
have already noticed a relationship between a meeting
beside a well and the theme of marriage (see pp. 7-11).
Jesus' words are thus not as incongruous as they might
seem at first sight. But the meaning of his request becomes even clearer if we remember that, unlike many
other spiritual paths, the Bible never separates the quest
for God and life with our fellow human beings, but
rather unites the two more and more deeply. In Israel
of old, the covenant with the Lord was made concrete
by the commitment to walk in God's footsteps, in other
words to imitate God's behavior, above all by acts of
solidarity and justice in the life of society. The Gospel
message goes even further in this direction, showing us
that the most essential commandment is in fact two-
fold: love of God and love of neighbor are two faces of
one and the same coin. By helping our neighbor in need,
we come to the aid of Christ himself.

▶ *I tell you the truth, to the extent that you did it for one
of these, the least of my brothers and sisters, you did it
for me. (Matthew 25:40)*

✔ If, in the Synoptic Gospels, Jesus replies to the question concerning the greatest commandment by naming
two (Mark 12:28-31 and parallels), that is undoubtedly
because he is quoting scriptural texts. But already the fact
that he mentions **two** in reply to a question that asks only
for **one** is significant. Elsewhere the unity between the two
is explicitly affirmed. *"If someone says 'I love God,' and
hates his brother or sister, that person is a liar. A person
who does not love his brother or sister, whom he sees,
cannot love God, whom he does not see. This is the commandment we have received from him: whoever loves
God must also love his brothers and sisters."* (1 John 4:20-
21)

Consequently, as soon as the Samaritan woman
begins to walk along the road of spiritual thirst, Jesus'

jarring words send her back to her daily life, to her relationships with her fellows, beginning with the one who should be the closest of all to her. In this way he keeps religion from becoming a flight from reality, a way to turn one's back on an inhospitable world by finding refuge in the serene heights of spirituality. At the very beginning of the Bible, God asked Cain a question after he murdered his brother: *Where is your brother Abel?... What have you done?* (Genesis 4:9-10). And here, it is as if Jesus were saying to the woman who is searching: "Where is your husband; what have you done with him?"

? Does my faith in God make me closer to those around me or does it increase the distance?

13

"I have no husband," the woman replied. Jesus said to her, "You are right to say you have no husband. You have had five husbands, and the one you have now is not your husband. You have told the truth there."   (John 4:17-18)

This verse may be the most enigmatic one of the entire story. From a historical point of view, it seems implausible that a woman living in a small town in Samaria would have contracted five successive marriages. It is true that the word translated by "husband" is simply the word "man," so perhaps it is not necessary to assume that there were five actual marriages. Because of this difficulty, however, and the fact that marriage in the Bible has a symbolic meaning, an allegorical explanation of this detail has gained favor among scholars. We have seen that, in the eyes of the Jews, the Samaritans confused worship of the one true God with religious practices imported from other traditions; they were viewed as syncretists. Thus the author of the Books of Kings explains that the gods of five different nations were worshipped in Samaria:

The king of Assyria brought people from Babylon, Cuthah, Avva, Hamath and Sepharvaim and settled them in the towns of Samaria to replace the Israelites. (...) Each national group made its own gods and set them up in the shrines the people of Samaria had made at the high places. (2 Kings 17:24,29)

Following this logic, the woman with her five husbands would be a symbol of the Samaritan nation, called by Jesus to give up its idolatry and to return to the God of Israel in order to receive the living water.

This interpretation is certainly not impossible. But looking for the meaning of the story on that level alone would mean emptying it of all dramatic density and reducing it to a disembodied allegory. The Samaritan woman, who up to now had a distinctive personality, would all at once be turned into a mere symbol standing for something else. And this verse would then be a kind of foreign body in the logic of the narrative as a whole. So it is necessary to ask the question: before attributing significance to it on another level, what meaning could this detail have in the development of the story taken in itself?

The text tells us that the woman has had relations with a series of men, none of which was definitive. It is fairly evident that someone who constantly changes partners in this way is searching for something, something that they do not find. This kind of repetition witnesses to a frustration, a basic lack which is unable to be filled. Our psychologists would be happy to inform us that when we perform the same acts over and over again only to find ourselves inevitably dissatisfied at the end, it is time to stop and think things over. Such an obsession leads nowhere; to find what we are looking for, we need to break the circle and move to another level. In this respect, we could compare the situation of someone who enters a new conjugal relationship again and again with that of a woman who goes to the well each day to draw water, only to end up every evening with an empty bucket.

? Do the words of Jesus show us a way out of our inner prisons and the circles that we tend to create? What is that way?

Seen from this point of view, the words of Jesus appear as a provocation to cause his partner to reflect on the truth of her life. They invite her to go deeper. What is she really looking for? What is her deepest thirst? If she enters upon the road Jesus is opening for her, the offer of living water will not be something that runs parallel to her daily activities, to her "real" life, like those people who go to church on Sunday morning and live an entirely unrelated life during the rest of the week. Jesus wants to help the woman to discover an inner unity rooted in the depths of her being, to find that desire which gives meaning and consistency to the whole of human existence.

And the way Jesus acts here clearly shows that his basic intention is to assist and not to criticize her.

▶ *God did not send his Son into the world to judge the*
world, but so that the world might be saved through him.
(John 3:17)

We should notice that he does not say even one negative word to the woman. Instead of blaming her, twice
he praises her (*You are right... You have told the truth*)!
Do we need clearer proof that what God wishes above
all is not to judge or condemn us, but to make us aware
of the truth of our life, so that we can change what
needs to be changed in order to receive the living water he constantly offers us?

14

The woman said to him, "Sir, I see that you
are a prophet. Our ancestors worshiped on
this mountain. But you say that the place
where people have to worship is in Jerusalem."

(John 4:19-20)

The woman is obviously not in the least offended by
Jesus' words. On the contrary, they help her better to
understand the identity of the man who is speaking to
her. First a Jew, then someone who may be greater than
Jacob, and now a prophet, in other words someone sent
by God to reveal the divine will. All of a sudden, the
conversation takes a more explicitly religious turn. The
Samaritan woman wants to take advantage of the presence of this man of God to get answers to her questions in this area.

It is significant that the first question that spontaneously comes to her mind concerns the differences between the religious traditions of humanity. Understanding these differences has evidently always been a problem, and things have not changed that much today. How many times do we hear on the lips of people, young or not-so-young, the question, "What are the differences between Catholics, Protestants, and Orthodox?" Or between Christians, Muslims, Buddhists...? If religious differences are problematic, it is equally true that this way of posing the question runs the risk of quickly leading to a dead end. Not only does it emphasize what divides, but in addition such a question implicitly looks for an answer of the sort: "X is wrong and Y is right." This kind of answer makes the separation between groups even more hard-and-fast. Religious truth is by its nature divisive, or so it would seem. It is almost impossible to reconcile, in human terms, the claims of truth and those of communion. This general and somewhat abstract statement is borne out by the religious history of our planet, marked by wars and disputes of all kinds that find their justification, if not always their cause, in the attitude of human beings towards the Absolute.

15

Jesus said to her, "Believe me, woman, the hour is coming when you will worship the Father neither on this mountain nor in Jerusalem." (John 4:21)

Because of this situation, Jesus cannot truly reply to the woman's question without going beyond her way of asking it. *Neither on this mountain nor in Jerusalem*: by these words, Jesus indicates that the solution to the problem has to be found elsewhere, on another level which she cannot as yet even imagine.

To understand these and the following words correctly, we must realize that Jesus employs the word "worship" in a much broader and deeper sense than the woman does. She uses it to refer to the religious duty of going to a holy place to make offerings and recite prayers to the deity; she remains on a practical level, thinking about where to go and what to do. Jesus, for his part, has in mind the global attitude of human beings toward God, made concrete in what they do and the way they live. If we understand this, we can more easily grasp the logic of this conversation. Jesus began by asking the woman to do something, then he told her an important secret, namely that the important thing was not to **do** but to **receive**. Since God is above all the Wellspring of life (indicated in this verse by the word "*Father*"), what matters most of all is recognizing the Giver and welcoming the Gift. And now the question of human activity comes up again, but only at this stage of the story is it finally placed in the right context: it is seen as the human **response** to God's gift. That is what Jesus means by worshiping God: to make one's life a response to the One who fills us with all good things.

How, then, can we worship God correctly? Jesus begins his reply with a play on words that sets us on the right path. *"Believe me...."* In other words, it is only trust in him that will give us the solution to this apparently insoluble problem. Jesus is the only one who knows the road towards true worship. It should be mentioned in passing that the expression *"woman"* used by Jesus is a title of respect; it also refers to the fact that the words of Jesus are not only addressed to one individual but to humanity as a whole, seen as God's counterpart.

> ✔ In the prophetic books, the figure of a woman often stands for the holy nation, God's partner (see Jeremiah 31:15; Hosea 3:1; Zephaniah 3:14; Isaiah 66:7ff). In key dialogues of the Fourth Gospel—with the Samaritan woman (John 4:21), with Mary of Magdala (20:13,15) and especially with his mother (2:4; 19:26)—Jesus addresses the one to whom he speaks with the title "Woman." And each time the person addressed has a significance that goes far beyond her individuality. There is also the Woman clothed with the sun in chapter 12 of the Book of Revelation. The only exception to this is perhaps John 8, the account of the woman caught in adultery, and this would be another indication that this story does not originally come from the Johannine circle.

"The hour is coming": access to this other level, where the divisions of humanity are overcome and where human beings enter into an authentic relationship with God, is linked to the coming of an "hour." In John's Gospel, the presence of the Son of God in the world as a human being is not a static reality that never evolves; it opens a way leading towards a fulfillment which Jesus calls "the hour" or "my hour." Until that hour has come, Jesus cannot fully reveal his powers

▶ *Jesus said to his mother, "What has this to do with me, woman? My hour has not yet come." (John 2:4)*

but paradoxically, the forces of evil cannot yet be fully unleashed against him.

▶ *So they attempted to seize him, but no one laid a hand on him, because his hour had not yet come. (John 7:30; see also 8:20)*

Later, when he goes up to Jerusalem towards the end of his public life and receives the homage of some non-Jews, he says:

The hour has come for the Son of Man to be glorified. (John 12:23)

The hour in question is thus the hour of his glorification, in other words, in John's vocabulary, of the full revelation of his identity. This comes about, however, in quite an unusual fashion:

I tell you the truth, unless the grain of wheat falls into the earth and dies, it remains a single grain. But if it dies, it bears much fruit. (John 12:24)

Jesus will reveal his true identity as the Son by giving his life to the end, like the seed that disappears beneath the earth.

Then, during the Last Supper, we read:

Before the feast of Passover, Jesus, knowing that his hour had come to pass out of this world to the Father, having loved his own who were in the world, loved them to the end. (John 13:1)

Jesus' hour is thus, in addition, the hour of his "passover," the act by which he crosses over from this world to the Father. And it is the hour when Jesus shows the fullness of his love. Finally, in his last prayer he says:

Father, the hour has come. Glorify your Son, so that your Son can glorify you and that, just as you gave him authority over all flesh, he can give eternal life to all those you have given to him. (John 17:1-2)

This hour is also the hour when the Father will be glorified, in other words, when the definitive and concrete answer will be given to the question "who is God?" At the same time, it is the hour when Jesus will give the fullness of life to all those who come to him.

This overview of the texts in John's Gospel dealing with the hour of Jesus shows clearly that the expression does not refer to something indicated on the dial of a clock. It is rather John's way of speaking of the definitive gift of his life which Jesus accomplishes through an act of total trust in his Father, in order to bring salvation to the human race. For Saint John, when all is said and done, Jesus' hour is equivalent to the paschal mystery, the cross and the resurrection viewed as two sides of one and the same reality.

If Jesus, then, mentions his "hour" in reply to the woman's question concerning the right way to worship God, that is because he wants to go beyond the level of abstract and theoretical considerations and point to an **event** as the solution. This event, which has already begun in her life although she does not yet realize it (*"it is here now,"* 4:23a), is the encounter with the crucified and risen Christ. The Gospel-writer thus wants us to see that it is in Jesus, and above all in the mystery of his death and resurrection, that we will discover how to respond to God adequately, beyond all the differences between human beings due to our necessarily partial ways of understanding reality.

16

You worship what you do not know. We worship what we know, for salvation comes from the Jews.   (John 4:22)

Jesus interrupts the main thrust of his words by a short parenthesis. To say that there is a path beyond the religious differences of humanity does not at all imply that everything is on the same level. Unlike so many of our contemporaries, Jesus does not claim that "all religions are the same." He is Jewish not just by an accident of birth, but by a divine decree which he assumes consciously and willingly. He considers the history of the people of Israel as a providential preparation for his coming, as a progressive revelation of the authentic face of God. At the same time, he does not say that other nations—here the Samaritans—are absolutely wrong. He simply points out that, although they worship the same Reality as the Jews, they do not have the same knowledge of it. In this way Jesus warns us against a simplistic view of the religious history of the human race. There are differences between traditions that need to be taken into account. Although God is indeed the God of all human beings, he does not act in the same way with each person, or with each people.

17

But the hour is coming—and it is here now—
when true worshipers will worship the Father
in spirit and truth. For the Father is seeking
worshipers who will worship him in that way.
God is spirit, and those who worship him have
to worship in spirit and truth.   (John 4:23-24)

Now we are back to the main argument. All these differences, whatever their importance on their own level,
are in fact relative with respect to the "hour" of Jesus.
This hour has a paradoxical aspect: although it is something that is on its way, at the same time it is already
present for the woman in the "now" of her encounter
with Jesus. It would perhaps be more exact to say that
the hour of Jesus is always present *here now* as a reality
that is coming, because it is a **Passover**. It can never be
possessed, held on to as something static; all we can do
is enter into its wake and let ourselves be borne onward.

❱ *Thanks be to God, who always leads us in a victory
procession in Christ and is spreading everywhere the fra-
grance of knowledge of him through us. (2 Corinthians
2:14)*

Jesus' hour is that of *true worshipers*. In John's
Gospel, the term "true" does not so much stand in opposition to "false" as it does to "incomplete." Here, it
refers back to the previous verse: a true worshiper is
someone who responds to God with full awareness, and
not in a partial, unconscious or involuntary fashion.
Who are these worshipers? Jesus tells us that they are

those who worship *in spirit and truth*. An understanding of this expression is thus the key to grasping the correct meaning of Jesus' words.

At this point we come up against a problem that we always confront when we try to understand the Bible, or indeed any text arising from another culture. We are always tempted to understand the meaning of a word, an expression or a narrative in function of our present situation. This procedure is not too serious when the chronological, cultural, intellectual or spiritual distance between us and the text is fairly short. But in other situations, it can lead us far astray.

The phrase we are currently examining, *to worship in spirit and truth*, is a very good example of this danger. Most of our contemporaries would spontaneously understand the expression in the following way: "My relationship with God is true if I am sincere, if my prayer comes from my heart and is not a mere outward rite." Or again: "The particular church I belong to is of little importance. What matters are my good intentions and the integrity of my heart."

However laudable, and even edifying, such sentiments may be, upon closer examination it is obvious that they have almost nothing to do with the Gospel according to Saint John. It would even be true to say that they lead us off on a tangent, far away from what Jesus is trying to get his conversation partner to understand. The only way to get back to the true path, then, is not to look at the meaning these words have for us today but to situate them within the general outlook of John's Gospel.

Let us begin with the term **spirit**. For John, the spirit is not the inside of a person as opposed to exterior and material realities; it does not refer to the realm of human thoughts or aspirations. The following phrase gives us the correct interpretation: *God is spirit*. Here, the spirit stands for the reality of God which transcends the realities of the world here below, the domain of creation and history, the human condition which John, following the Hebrew Scriptures, sometimes refers to as "flesh." And since everything in God is personal, and the personification of this "spiritual" aspect of God is the person we call the Holy Spirit, we can say that here the term "spirit" stands for the reality of God in general, and the Holy Spirit in particular.

▶ *Jesus replied, "I tell you the truth, if a person is not born of water and spirit, they cannot enter the Kingdom of God. What is born of flesh is flesh, and what is born of spirit is spirit." (John 3:5-6)*

▶ *"The spirit is what gives life; the flesh can accomplish nothing. The words I have spoken to you are spirit, and they are life." (John 6:63)*

Next, **truth**. This term has a specific meaning in the Fourth Gospel. The truth is not something abstract, some kind of theoretical knowledge, nor is it a synonym for sincerity of heart as opposed to hypocrisy and falsehood. The word here refers specifically to the truth about God's identity and designs. In the Fourth Gospel, "the truth" is the correct answer, an answer which is existential and not abstract, to two questions, "Who is God?" and "What does God want to accomplish for and with us?" And for Saint John, it is the life or, more accurately, the life as it is recapitulated in the death-and-resurrection of Jesus the Christ that offers the definitive answer to these questions. That is why Jesus can proclaim without hesitation: *"I am the truth"* (John 14:6).

To sum up, the spirit stands for God, and

specifically the Holy Spirit. Truth is God's self-revelation through Jesus Christ. **Now it is not by chance that these are the two basic meanings we found for the living water promised to the Samaritan woman!** In other words, the only way to worship in spirit and truth is to receive from Jesus this gift of living water. It is literally impossible to do this by our own powers, by acts of self-discipline or an abundance of good will. To be the partner that God is seeking, there is no other way than to enter into a relationship with Jesus, the one who is in communion with the Father from all eternity,

▶ *See John 1:1; 10:30; 17:5*

so that he can bring us in our turn into this communion.

▶ *See John 1:12; 14:1-3.23; 17:26*

Expressed in a positive manner, it is by receiving from Jesus the gift of living water that we become true worshipers, beings who respond to God appropriately. In a play on words which is in fact much more than that, by **responding** authentically we become believers who are **responsible**, who act with full awareness. This is a key theme in the New Testament. Both Saint Paul and Saint John speak about it, although each employs a different image to do so.

Saint Paul, for his part, describes the progression towards the status of a responsible believer as the transition from childhood to adulthood. The significance of this image is somewhat obscured by the fact that in the Gospels, Jesus speaks of children in an overwhelmingly positive way.

▶ *Jesus said, "Let the little children come to me; do not hinder them, for God's Kingdom belongs to such as these.*

*I tell you the truth, only those who welcome the King-
dom of God like a child will ever enter it." (Mark 10:14-
15; read also Luke 9:46-48)*

For Jesus, children are beings who know they cannot
go forward solely by their own powers; they have a vi-
tal need to trust in others. But in Paul's writings, the
metaphor is looked at from a different angle. The
apostle starts from the fact that children are not able
to act on their own; they follow directives that come
from without. In other words, they are not self-actual-
ized but have to follow others more or less blindly:

*What I am saying is, as long as the heir is still a minor,
he is no different from a slave, though he is the legal owner
of all the property. He is subject to guardians and admin-
istrators until the time set by his father. In the same way,
when we were under age, we were enslaved to the elements
of the world.* (Galatians 4:1-3)

Christ came to save us from this situation and to
make possible a true filial relationship with God by the
inner gift of the Spirit.

*But when the day finally arrived, God sent his Son, born
of a woman, born subject to the Law, to redeem those subject to the Law, so that we might become God's [fully
mature] sons and daughters. And as you are sons and
daughters, God sent into our hearts the Spirit of his Son
who cries out: Abba, Father!* (Galatians 4:4-6)

And yet it is up to us to enter into this new life
that God offers to us. Otherwise we remain immature:

*My brothers and sisters, I was not able to speak to you as
spiritual people but as unspiritual ones [literally: of the*

*flesh], as people still immature in Christ. I gave you milk
to drink, not solid food, because you were not yet able to
take it. And now you are still not able, for you are still
unspiritual. As long as there continues to be jealousy and
quarrels among you, are you not unspiritual and is your
behavior not merely human?* (1 Corinthians 3:1-3)

▶ *See also 1 Corinthians 13:11; 14:20*

The letter to the Ephesians explains that this transition to adulthood is not simply something that happens to an isolated individual but rather to the Body of
Christ as a whole, to the entire community of believers:

*...until we all reach unity in the faith and in knowledge of
the Son of God, forming the perfect Man, mature with the
fullness of Christ. Then we will no longer be children, tossed
and carried about by every wind of teaching.... But speaking the truth in love, we will grow up in all respects into the
one who is the Head, Christ.* (Ephesians 4:13-15)

✔ In all of the above texts Saint Paul uses the Greek word
nēpios, which can be translated "child" but which has
the specific nuance, especially in a legal context, of "immature person, minor, someone not yet of age."

Saint John, in his turn, makes use of a different
image to say the same thing:

*I no longer call you slaves, because a slave does not know
what his master is doing. I call you friends, because I have
made known to you everything I have heard from my Father.* (John 15:15)

In short, to receive from Jesus the gift of living
water means leaving behind the status of a minor or a

slave to be an adult believer who knows what he or she is doing and who chooses it freely. It means being a friend of Jesus, a person whose behavior is dictated not by orders and motivations that are extrinsic to the matter at hand, such as the fear of punishment or the hope for a reward, but by friendship, a spontaneous impulse that arises from the bottom of one's heart.

> **?** Does the spirit of childhood of which the Gospel speaks contradict the need for an adult faith? What keeps us from being "true worshipers" of God?

And Jesus tells us something unheard of in this respect: *the Father is seeking worshipers who will worship him in that way* (John 4:23b). In the Bible and especially in John's writings, the verb "to seek" generally has a strong meaning. Most of the time, it describes the behavior of someone filled with a longing for the fullness of life.

▶ *O God... earnestly I seek you; my soul thirsts for you, my body longs for you (Psalm 63:1; compare Psalms 42:1-2; 84:2)*

▶ *My soul yearns for you in the night; in the morning my spirit longs for you.... (Isaiah 26:9)*

And when some people begin to follow Jesus at the beginning of his ministry, he asks them the question: "What are you seeking?" (John 1:38)

▶ *See also John 6:26; 20:15*

But here, it is not a human being but God who is seeking. According to Jesus, God is the one who is filled with the desire to find a counterpart able to welcome the life he can give, someone who can respond to him on the same level. The notion of a God who goes looking for

"friends," who is longing for an authentic encounter
with those he has created, is quite surprising, to say the
least. This way of seeing is very different from the image of the divinity that we spontaneously conceive. Left
to ourselves, we tend rather to envisage a god who fills
in the gaps, who is there to satisfy our needs (the in-
fantile stage) or else, when our rationality gains the
upper hand, a deity who may be benevolent but who
is in the final analysis indifferent to the world here below. These are not, however, the God the Bible reveals.
On the contrary, the Bible is the history of a God who,
animated by a foolhardy love, "leaves home" and sets
out in search of his creatures in order to elevate them
to an authentic communion with himself.

▶ *The Lord God called to the man, "Where are you?"*
(Genesis 3:9)

? What changes in my life when I realize that God has
been searching for me even before I began to look for him?

If the essential thing, in order to enter into a true
relationship with God, is to receive from Jesus the gift
of living water, then human limitations are no longer
an obstacle and as a result a unity among human beings is possible. In this way Jesus, indirectly but nonetheless truly, offers the response to the problem of
human diversity mentioned above. What brings us into
a relationship with God is not something rooted in our
human nature; it is not the fruit of effort or an accident of birth; it is a pure gift offered to all. Here we
are at the opposite extreme from the logic of the trea-
sure-hunt with its inevitable retinue of competition,
jealousy and division. Since the heart of the matter is
an utterly free gift, human differences can subsist within
a more encompassing communion, rooted in God.

When confronted with Jesus and the living water he offers, the important thing is no longer to try and decide who is wrong and who is right, but simply to accept the gift that reconciles us.

18

The woman said to him, "I know that the Messiah is coming, the one they call Christ. When he comes, he will explain everything to us." Jesus said to her, "I am [he], the one speaking to you." (John 4:25-26)

The words of Jesus, rooted in the absolute of God, inevitably go beyond the comprehension we have of them; they are an invitation to set out on a journey. So it is not surprising that the woman's first attempt is rather to bring Jesus' words into harmony with her own expectations, those which come from the religious tradition to which she belongs. In the books of Moses, which the Samaritans hold to be inspired, we find this oracle:

The Lord your God will raise up for you a prophet like me from among your own people. You must listen to this prophet. (...) The Lord said to me: "I will raise up for them a prophet like you from among their people, and I will put my words in that prophet's mouth. My prophet will tell them everything I command." (Deuteronomy 18:15, 18)

The woman thus is not thinking primarily of a
royal Messiah, a descendant of David, but of a new
prophet like Moses, someone who will fully reveal
God's designs. By the simplest words possible (*I am [he]*,
the one speaking to you), Jesus expresses the link between
himself and the centuries-old longing of the Samaritan
people. He has come not just to fulfill the hopes of the
Jewish people, but all the desires for fulfillment placed
by God in the hearts of his creatures. To fulfill means
to satisfy and to fill beyond all expectations: the expression *ego eimi*, "I am [the one]," is in addition the biblical way of expressing the ineffable Name of God.

❯ *God said to Moses, "I AM WHO I AM. This is what you are
to say to the Israelites: 'I AM has sent me to you.'" (Exodus
3:14)*

❯ *You are my witnesses, declares the Lord,
and my servant whom I have chosen,
so that you may know and believe me
and understand that I AM he.
Before me no god was formed,
nor will there be one after me.
I, even I am the Lord,
and apart from me there is no savior.
(Isaiah 43:10-11)*

If Jesus is indeed the longed-for Messiah, he is in fact
much more: in him, the absolute Wellspring of all being becomes fully present within the created universe.

19

At that moment his disciples came, and they were astonished that he was talking to a woman. None of them said, however, "What are you looking for?" or "Why are you talking with her?"   (John 4:27)

All of a sudden, the scene changes. With the arrival of the disciples, the private conversation with the woman comes to an end; she goes off to find the townspeople while Jesus stays with his disciples. The separation between Jews and Samaritans is temporarily re-established in preparation for the grand finale when all will be together. In the meantime, two short episodes take place simultaneously which situate both groups within the reconciling plan of God.

Let us look first at the way things develop on the side of the Jews. The dominant attitude is one of incomprehension. It may indeed be true to say that *salvation comes from the Jews* (John 4:22); nevertheless, this people which is the bearer of salvation is in no way privileged with respect to others regarding its understanding of the treasure it is conserving for the world. The Bible is clear about this, and yet it in no way justifies an attitude of hostility toward the chosen people. On the contrary, it warns all of us against any arrogance or self-sufficiency. Contact with others is necessary so that we ourselves may become aware of the gifts we have received. Communicating the faith is never a one-way street; in accomplishing their mission, those who evangelize are evangelized in their turn. And any qualities

which can only be maintained at the price of separation have little to do with the progress of the Gospel.

In this narrative, then, the disciples of Jesus will
need the witness of the Samaritans in order to enter
fully into the mystery of their Master, though he is a
Jew like them, and into the designs of God which he
reveals. This is what Saint Paul tries to explain in chap-
ters 9-11 of his letter to the Romans: the crisis brought
about by the entry of the Gentiles into an intimate relationship with the God of Israel was necessary to make
his compatriots aware of the utmost consequences of
their faith. Or as Jesus himself explained in the well-
known story of the prodigal son, without the departure
and the return of the younger son, his older brother,
though he himself had never left home, would never
have been brought to a full understanding of his situation and his relationship with his father.

▶ *Read Luke 15:11-32*

> **?** How have people whom I helped helped me in turn?
> What have we received from those with whom we shared
> our faith by word or deed?

At this stage in the story, the disciples are once
again bewildered by the behavior of their Teacher. At
the same time, they do not dare question him. In their
relationship with him they do not yet have that
parrhēsia, that freedom of speech, that joyous confidence which flows from the mutuality of love. In short,
they are not yet, in John's meaning of the term, Jesus'
friends.

▶ *John 15:15*

In this verse, the Gospel-writer uses one of his

customary plays on words. Without expressing it aloud, the disciples mentally ask Jesus, *"What are you looking for?"* That is the same verb which was used in verse 23 to speak of the Father's activity. By entering into a conversation with the Samaritan woman, Jesus is truly in the image of his Father. He goes looking for friends; he wants to find partners who are able to enter fully into a common Life.

20

In the meantime, the disciples urged him, saying, "Rabbi, eat." But he said to them, "I have food to eat of which you are unaware." So the disciples said to one another, "Could someone have brought him something to eat?" Jesus said to them, "My food is to do the will of the One who sent me and to bring his work to completion." (John 4:31-34)

At this point, Jesus and his disciples have an exchange of words quite characteristic of the Fourth Gospel. It cannot truly be called a dialogue, because the disciples' comprehension is practically nonexistent. Jesus speaks from a place which is his and the disciples are somewhere else; they understand and reply on an entirely different level. In John's language, he is from above, they are from below.

▶ *You are from below; I am from above. You are of this world; I am not of this world. (John 8:23)*

▶ *The one who comes from above is above all; the one who is of the earth belongs to the earth and speaks in an earthly way. (John 3:31)*

On account of this disparity, no true encounter takes place. The exchange of words serves only to emphasize the originality of Jesus' message and the need for a *metanoia* in order to enter into his outlook. In comparison with this abortive dialogue, Jesus' conversation with the Samaritan woman comes across as all the more exceptional: with her forthrightness, she is one of the only persons in John's Gospel who is able to enter into Jesus' perspective—although from afar—and to go forward with him.

In these verses, the conversation circles around the theme of food, a theme obviously parallel to that of water. Here there is a contrast between the food which the disciples want to give their Teacher and his real food which they are unaware of; previously, the text had emphasized the contrast between the water from the well and the living water which Jesus alone can give. The disciples' misconception serves above all to emphasize the saying in verse 34, which is literally mind-boggling. Whereas, as a general rule, activity consumes energy and so we require nourishment in order to work more, Jesus reveals here that what nourishes him is **doing** something; he is fed by working! He thus has an activity that is at the same time a source of life and energy—doing the will of the Father who sent him into the world. And what is that will? Fortunately, another text from the Gospel puts it clearly:

I have come down from heaven not to do my own will but the will of the One who sent me. And the will of the One

*who sent me is this: that I should not lose anyone he has
given to me, but raise that person up on the last day. For
this is the will of my Father, that whoever looks upon the
Son and believes in him may have eternal life, and I will
raise that person up on the last day.* (John 6:38-40)

God's will, which is a source of life and energy for
Jesus, is to communicate the fullness of life to human
beings, to bring them with him from death to life in
God. In addition, the verb used in the second part of
John 4:34, "to perfect, bring to completion" (*teleioûn*)
and its cognates (*telein, telos*), often evoke for Saint John
the definitive gift of his life which Jesus accomplishes
on the cross.

◗ *Before the feast of Passover Jesus, knowing that his hour
had come to pass over from this world to the Father, having loved his own who were in the world, loved them to
the very end* (eis telos). *(John 13:1)*

◗ *I have glorified you on earth, bringing to completion
(*teleiōsas*) the work that you gave me to do. (John 17:4)*

By means of this supreme gift, he communicates the
Spirit, God's own life, to humanity. In the act of dying, he becomes a source of living water.

◗ *...knowing that all things had already been brought to
completion* (tetelestai), *in order that the Scriptures might
be fulfilled* (teleiōthēi), *Jesus said: I am thirsty.... When
he had taken the vinegar he said: It is completed
(*tetelestai*), and bowing his head he handed over the
spirit.... One of the soldiers pierced his side with a lance,
and all of a sudden blood and water came out. (John
19:28, 30, 34)*

In other words, the hunger and thirst that Jesus
experiences is his desire to give us the living water, so

that we can be true worshipers of the Father and so that unity among human beings becomes possible. When he finds women and men who are ready and willing to listen to him and to receive the gift he offers, his thirst is quenched, his hunger satisfied. Earlier, we interpreted Jesus' thirst as a mark of his solidarity with the human condition. At this point, we discover an even deeper significance. This thirst is, in the final analysis, an expression of the search that the Father ceaselessly undertakes (John 4:23), of God's desire to transmit his own life to human beings.

▶ *God loved the world so much that he gave his only Son, so that whoever believes in him would not perish, but have eternal life. (John 3:16)*

The words spoken by Jesus on the cross, *I am thirsty* (John 19:28) bespeak a will to give himself that is without bounds, which does not even stop at death. As long as there are beings who do not know the Father, this thirst remains. If we want to say with Saint John "*God is love*" (1 John 4:8,16), we must immediately add that this love is utterly different from a vapid benevolence. At the heart of the mystery of God we encounter a burning fire, the passion of a self-giving. There is nothing indifferent in God; he throws himself fully into the adventure of his creation, holding nothing back, going all the way so that nothing will be lost. Judged according to human criteria, God is not reasonable. God is crazy with love.

▶ *Read 1 Corinthians 1:18-31*

21

The woman then left her bucket and went back to the town. She said to the people, "Come and see a man who told me everything I did! Could he possibly be the Messiah?" They left the town and came to him.

(John 4:28-30)

While Jesus is speaking with his disciples, the woman goes back to town to find her compatriots. She has thus entered the final stage of the journey of faith, that of communicating to others what she herself has experienced. Some would say that she has become an **evangelist** or an **evangelizer**, a bringer of good news.

▶ *How beautiful on the mountains*
are the feet of those who bring good news,
who proclaim peace,
who bring good tidings,
who proclaim salvation,
who say to Zion:
Your God reigns!
(Isaiah 52:7)

Others would even call her an **apostle**, although she has not been explicitly sent by Jesus.

✔ If we wanted to apply the title apostle ("someone who is sent out") at all costs to a woman, Mary of Magdala would be a much better candidate. The Risen Christ said to her, "*Go to my brothers and tell them....*" (John 20:17). In fact, the Eastern Church still refers to Mary of Magdala as the "apostle to the apostles."

But the expression "witness" would be more in accord with Saint John's outlook. Those who have seen God's glory in Jesus are led to **bear witness** to it before others.

▶ *See John 1:7-8; 15:27; 19:35; 21:24; 1 John 1:2*

To be a witness, it is not enough to have seen and heard something; witnesses must also assume responsibility for what they have seen and heard, in other words be ready to answer for it. Witnesses take their stand on the truth of what they have grasped and, in this way, they enable what was hidden to take its place in public life, to appear in the light of day.

The journey of faith is not complete until this dimension of witnessing appears, this movement towards others. At the same time, in order to bear witness it is not necessary to have understood everything, to be an expert in theology, to have overcome all forms of doubt. Witnesses simply have to communicate what they themselves have grasped, no matter how rudimentary it may seem. Later in his Gospel, in telling a story of a man born blind, Saint John gives us a marvelous example of this. The man healed by Jesus says, *"I don't know whether he is a sinner or not. I only know one thing: I was blind and now I can see"* (John 9:25). Similarly, the Samaritan woman does not attempt to instruct her fellow citizens from a position of superiority; she simply tells them how Jesus has entered her life and the consequences of that event.

? What aspects of the Gospel message can I put into practice in the different areas of my life? What have I received that I can give to others?

When she goes to find the others, the woman leaves her bucket beside the well. What is the significance of this detail? Let us begin with the logic of the narrative itself. At present, in her haste to share her experience with others, the woman goes straight to the goal; she leaves behind all that could weigh or slow her down. She does not even think any longer about the reason why she had previously come to the well. She has found another reason for being, a much more important one, which calls upon all her energies. This detail implies, on a still deeper level, an implicit trust in the words of Jesus: the bucket has now become superfluous since she no longer needs to come to the well to draw water and to keep it. Abandoned beside the well, this container remains as a symbol of the old life she has left behind.

▶ *...they entered the tomb and saw the linen bands lying there and the cloth which had covered his face, not lying with the linen bands but folded up in a separate place. (John 20:6b-7)*

In the story of the call of the first disciples we see something similar:

Walking by the Sea of Galilee, Jesus saw Simon and Andrew, Simon's brother, casting their nets into the sea; they were fishermen. Jesus said to them: "Come with me and I will make you fishers of people." And at once they left their nets and followed him. (Mark 1:16-18)

Here, the transition between the disciples' previous existence as fishermen and the call to become *fishers of people* is indicated by leaving the nets behind. What was essential beforehand is now revealed to be superfluous. This shows us the authentic significance of Gospel simplicity: being a companion of Jesus implies a continuous simplification of life, not because we are forced to or out of a sense of obligation, but because a relationship with him and faith in his words engender a confident trust which is the source of greater freedom. Assured of the living water which will never run dry and desiring to make room for it, we can leave behind all those realities which previously filled our lives and from which we looked in vain for security and true satisfaction.

? What do the bucket and the nets represent in my life?

In mentioning that the Samaritan woman came to the well at noon, we suggested that one reason for this was that she wanted to avoid meeting other people; she was perhaps looked down upon because of her behavior. If this interpretation is justified, then the change that has come about is extremely important: now she runs **toward** the others to spread the good news. The encounter with Jesus restores the relationship between her and her contemporaries. We thus see how inward reconciliation takes concrete shape in reconciliation with others. And then, through the witness of the woman, the townspeople are led to leave behind their ordinary routine in order to set out on the road toward Jesus. Saint John wants us to realize here that witnesses do not try to attract others to themselves, but solely to Christ.

✔ In John's Gospel, this theme is especially clear in the life of the Baptizer. Read John 1:6-8,19-34; 3:28-30.

22

Do you not say: Four months more, and then the harvest? Well, I tell you: lift up your eyes and look at the fields, they are white for the harvest. Already the harvester is earning his wages and bringing in fruit for eternal life, so that the sower might rejoice together with the harvester. For this proves the saying: one person sows, another person harvests. I sent you to harvest what you did not work for. Other people did the work, and you are reaping the benefits of their toil.   (John 4:35-38)

When he sees the Samaritans coming towards him, Jesus changes the subject and speaks to his disciples about the harvest. In the Bible and in the Jewish tradition, this image is sometimes used to indicate a fulfillment. For instance, a text from the prophet Isaiah speaks about the Day of the Lord, when the scattered nation will be gathered together once again:

In that day the Lord will thresh from the flowing Euphrates to the Wadi of Egypt, and you, O Israelites, will be gathered up one by one. (Isaiah 27:12)

After the hard work, there will come the joy of gathering in the fruit. It is not surprising, then, that the harvest becomes a ready-made image to represent the Kingdom of God present in fullness. This is true in

Jesus' own preaching. Sometimes, as in Jewish thought, he uses it to refer to a future reality:

Let both grow together until the harvest. Then at harvest-time I will say to the harvesters: first collect the weeds and tie them in bundles for burning, then gather together the wheat and bring it into my barn. (Matthew 13:30)

But in other sayings of Jesus, the harvest refers to an event that is happening right now, and this is more in conformity with the newness of the Gospel. Through the coming of Christ, God's Reign already mysteriously enters the world here below:

The harvest is abundant, but the workers are few. So ask the harvest-master to send out workers into his field. (Luke 10:2)

In the Gospel according to Saint John, the harvest is above all a present reality. But in that Gospel, it is manifested by **signs** that can seem tiny, even insignificant, in human terms. Here, the inhabitants of a small town in Samaria come to Jesus. At another moment, a handful of Greeks want to see him.

▶ *John 12:20-21*

And each time, Jesus' response can appear out of proportion to the event, because in these seemingly trivial happenings he sees the coming of God's Kingdom, a universal reconciliation with God and among human beings that is in the process of becoming reality. For Saint John, Jesus is not the one who is mistaken about the significance of the events; rather, it is we who are called to discover a new way of looking. We are invited to look beneath the surface of things and to perceive

them as signs of God's glory, signs of the universe transformed into a world of justice and peace. That is why,
here as elsewhere, Jesus insists so strongly on the need
to see: *Well, I tell you: lift up your eyes and look at the
fields!* Stop acting like sleepwalkers; a whole new world
is at your door!

> **?** How can we acquire a new way of looking that en-
> ables us to see, in every act of reconciliation, justice or
> forgiveness, a sign of God's Kingdom making its way in
> the world?

What makes it a bit more difficult to comprehend
these verses is that Jesus emphasizes in turn different
and complementary aspects of the work of harvesting,
so we could easily have the impression that he is con-
tradicting himself. First of all (verses 35-36) he speaks
about it as something that is already taking place. That
is because in him God's Reign has come down to earth,
even if our eyes of flesh do not yet see anything, or at
most small and apparently insignificant signs. Harvest-
time is already here, a time of unspeakable joy. Nevertheless, the advent of the Kingdom personified in Jesus
does not eliminate the fact that it comes into being by
stages, both in the history of humankind as well as in
our personal lives. So in repeating the proverb about
the difference between the sower and the person who
harvests (verses 37-38), Jesus completes what he first
said. The realization of God's plan involves a dimension of patience: there is the long period of preparation
in the history of the tiny nation of Israel, the coming of
Jesus as a man on earth, then the continuation of his
work in the existence of the community of his disciples,
the Christian Church. The disciples—and John is thinking also (or especially) of those for whom he is writing,
several decades after Christ's death—harvest the fruit

of Jesus' efforts, of his self-giving to the very end. In the logic of the story, the disciples, by entering into a relationship with the Samaritans, benefit from the activity of Jesus and the woman. More generally, we all build upon the foundations of those who went before us, and this goes as well for communion among human beings.

In analogous fashion, in the life of every believer, the growth of the inner life takes place in successive stages, too. Even if everything is given at the beginning in the yes of baptism, the long patience of an entire lifetime is needed for the seed to bear its fruit. Believers go through times when they see almost no tangible signs, when they journey in sheer trust with no visible support, and then all of a sudden they realize anew, as if for the first time, the value of the life they are living. Fulfillment is not so much something added on to what we have as the sudden awareness of the value of the life we are **already** living in the midst of uncertainties and ambiguities: *Were not our hearts burning within us while he spoke to us on the road...?* (Luke 24:32).

23

Many of the Samaritans from that town believed in him because of what the woman said when she testified, "He told me everything I ever did." So when the Samaritans came to him, they asked him to stay with them. And

he stayed there two days. Many more came
to believe on account of his words, and they
said to the woman, "We no longer believe on
account of what you said. Now we have heard
for ourselves, and we know that he is truly the
savior of the world." (John 4:39-42)

The story ends with a great closing celebration. For the
first time, everybody is present: Jesus and the woman,
the disciples and the townspeople.

✔ It is true that Saint John never mentions the presence
of the disciples in this final scene. He says only that **Jesus**
is invited by the Samaritans to stay with them. That is
undoubtedly because, on a theological level, human beings of different backgrounds enter into communion with
one another not "directly," but by opening themselves to
Christ. Without an explicit proof to the contrary, however,
it would be unwarranted to think that the disciples are
not implicitly included in the invitation extended to their
master.

In the first place, the Gospel-writer makes explicit the
procedure by which a person comes to faith, the different stages that have to be gone through, as he did
when he wrote about the call of the first disciples in
John 1:35-42. Normally, people hear about Jesus
through another believer who witnesses to what he or
she has discovered. The revelation of Jesus Christ does
not fall from the sky; it comes through the channel of
other human beings who in their turn received it from
others, going all the way back to the disciples who were
there *from the beginning.*

▶ *What was from the beginning, (...) what we saw and heard we proclaim to you, so that you too may be in communion with us. (1 John 1:1-4)*

? What women and men have awakened and sustained my faith in the course of my life?

Even if someone finds out about Jesus simply by reading the Bible, they must have received that book from other believers who passed it on, translated it and printed it. Whether we wish to admit it or not, when we come to the faith we take our place as a link in a living **tradition**.

✔ For many people, the word "tradition" is a synonym for an old habit or an outdated custom. It is therefore essential to recover the authentic meaning of the notion. The word comes from the Latin *tradere*, "to hand down or over." It refers to that continuity across the centuries linking us directly to the first Christians and to Christ himself.

But although the Christian faith is a tradition, a reality based on the testimony of others, it is no less true that it is not enough to believe by hearsay. An indirect encounter with Christ, by its very nature, must lead to a direct encounter which, if it is accepted, creates a communion, a sharing of life. Saint John expresses this by the verb "to stay, remain" (verse 40).

▶ *Jesus said, "Remain in me, as I in you. (...) Whoever remains in me, and I in them, will bear much fruit." (John 15:1-10)*

And then, like the Samaritans, believers reenact the experience of another person of faith centuries earlier, when he cried out to God after much suffering, *"I used to know you through others, but now I have a personal contact"* (cf. Job 42:5).

In describing the reaction of the Samaritans, the Gospel-writer wants to show us that the first generation of believers is in no way privileged with respect to those who come to the faith later on. Our relationship with Christ is no less direct than theirs; it is not a second-hand reality. To believe in the resurrection means knowing that Christ, by the power of the Holy Spirit, is present for us today in a manner that is no less real than it was two thousand years ago, even if he is not visible to our eyes of flesh.

▶ *Jesus said to Thomas: "You are a believer because you have seen me. Happy are those who believe without seeing!" (John 20:29)*

It is significant that the Samaritans tell the woman what they have understood about Christ. Earlier she was the one who witnessed to them, and now she receives **their** testimony. The evangelizer is evangelized in her turn. The story thus reminds us that faith is not communicated in one direction only. We all help one another to go forward on the road. There are no privileged people who possess the truth all by themselves: everyone has to rely on the support of others.

They asked [Jesus] to stay with them. The story ends in an astounding way: Samaritans invite a Jewish rabbi and his disciples, their hereditary enemies, to be their guests! This is a powerful sign of reconciliation, of communion, as we can easily understand if we replace the names of these two groups by other names from situations closer to us in time and space, in the Middle East, the Balkans, Africa, Northern Ireland.... At the beginning of the story the Jews, the disciples of Jesus, entered the town to buy some provisions; their relationship with the Samaritans was uniquely a commercial one, based on self-interest and profit. Now they are

guests of the Samaritans, and self-interest has given way
to the generosity of sharing. And that is only possible,
in the final analysis, because Jesus has come to give living water without cost to all who desire it. Once it has
begun to gush forth from the cross, this water overflows
until it becomes a wellspring of selfless love able to
transform all of human existence.

▶ *One of the soldiers pierced his side with a lance, and
all of a sudden blood and water came out. (John 19:34)*

It does not take a great deal of imagination to see
the last scene of this story, showing Jews and Samaritans together around Jesus and the woman, as a kind
of wedding celebration. Naturally the image is incongruous if taken literally, but it fits well with the stories
we have examined in the Hebrew Scriptures that tell
of encounters beside a well. In those cases, the story
always ended with a marriage. We know that, in the
biblical and Jewish tradition, a wedding banquet is a
classical image that evokes the definitive reconciliation
of humanity in the Kingdom of God.

▶ *On this mountain the Lord Almighty will prepare
a feast of rich food for all peoples,
a banquet of aged wine—
the best of meats and the finest of wines…
(Isaiah 25:6)*

▶ *Jesus again spoke to them in parables, saying, "The Kingdom of heaven is similar to a king who gave a wedding
banquet for his son.…" (Matthew 22:1-10)*

It is not for nothing that, in the Gospel according to
Saint John, the first sign that Jesus accomplishes is to
provide better wine for a wedding celebration, so that
he is mistaken for the bridegroom himself.

❱ *The steward called the bridegroom and said to him,
"Everybody serves the good wine first and then, when
people are drunk, the cheap stuff. You have kept the good
wine till now." (John 2:9b-10)*

And in the previous chapter, John the Baptist said:

*The bride belongs to the bridegroom. But the bridegroom's
friend, who stands there and hears him, is filled with joy
at the bridegroom's voice. That is the joy I feel, and it is
now complete.* (John 3:29)

Jesus is the bridegroom who has come to invite
human beings to enter into a shared life with him and,
through him, with the Father. When we welcome
Christ and drink his living water or his new wine, we
already are taking part in the *wedding of the Lamb* (Revelation 19:7-9; 21:2), in the joy of a reconciled world.
The Gospel-writer does not see this as only a future
reality, but rather as something already at work in the
existence of the Christian community, the Church,
where beings of the most variegated backgrounds are
brought together as one family. The final scene of our
story offers us a striking image of that Church, place of
universal solidarity and sharing, seed of a new humanity, transposition into this world of the divine communion.

❱ *What we saw and heard
we proclaim to you,
so that you too may be in communion with us.
And our communion is with the Father
and with his Son Jesus Christ.
We write these things to you
so that our joy may be complete.
(1 John 1:3-4)*

This universal note finds confirmation in the last
words of the passage. We have noted that one of the
main themes that run through the narrative is the question "Who is this man?" In the course of the conversation, the woman gives a series of replies in which she is
gradually better able to penetrate the mystery of the
man speaking to her: a Jew, someone who may be even
greater than Jacob, a prophet, perhaps the Messiah....
And then, implicitly, the true Bridegroom, the seventh
man to come into her life, the one who finally quenches
her thirst, stilling her obsessive quest by bringing it to
another level (see pp. 53-56)—in this he is an image of
the Sabbath, the seventh day that breaks the circle,
opening the week to a fulfillment in God. And now, at
the end, the Samaritans bring this line to its climax: *We
know that he is truly the savior of the world.*

In other words, Jesus offers living water to the
whole of humankind, and this water will turn them into
true worshipers of the Father *in spirit and truth.* By his
teaching and, still more, by the gift of his life, Christ
communicates full knowledge of God and of his designs,
a knowledge that leads to a sharing of life. And this
knowledge and this communion are not the exclusive
possession of one nation. Through Christ, a source of
reconciliation that is truly universal enters into the history of our planet. Although it is universal, this source
is at the same time personal, because it enters into the
heart of every person who comes to Jesus in a spirit of
openness. Furthermore, it is a source that is both inward and concrete, because it is already lived out in the
existence of the Christian community where, day after day, women and men try to live lives of reconciliation in the midst of the difficulties and the misunder-
standings of the society around them. From beginnings
that appear insignificant to our eyes of flesh, God en-

ters into the world to transform it from top to bottom.
A seemingly chance encounter beside a well in Samaria
is thus shown to be charged with consequences for the
entire universe.

> **?** Read Isaiah 6:1-8 and John 20:11-18. Compare the
> experience of Mary of Magdala and of the Samaritan
> woman: in what ways are they similar, and in what ways
> different? What makes Isaiah and Mary witnesses, or even
> evangelizers? To whom is God sending me? How can I
> bear witness to what I have experienced of God?

ST PAULS

This book was designed and published by ST PAULS/
Alba House, the publishing arm of the Society of St.
Paul, an international religious congregation of priests
and brothers dedicated to serving the Church through
the communications media. For information regarding
this and associated ministries of the Pauline Family of
Congregations, write to the Vocation Director, Society
of St. Paul, 7050 Pinehurst, Dearborn, Michigan 48126.
Phone (313) 582-3798 or check our internet site,
www.albahouse.org